Lectionary Stories For Preaching And Teaching

Series III, Cycle B

Keith Hewitt

CSS Publishing Company, Inc.
Lima, Ohio

Lectionary Stories for Preaching and Teaching

FIRST EDITION
Copyright © 2020
by CSS Publishing Co., Inc.

Published by CSS Publishing Company, Inc., Lima, Ohio 45807. All rights reserved. No part of this publication may be reproduced in any manner whatsoever without the prior permission of the publisher, except in the case of brief quotations embodied in critical articles and reviews. Inquiries should be addressed to: CSS Publishing Company, Inc., Permissions Department, 5450 N. Dixie Highway, Lima, Ohio 45807.

Library of Congress Cataloging-in-Publication Data: Pending

For more information about CSS Publishing Company resources, visit our website at www.csspub.com, email us at csr@csspub.com, or call (800) 241-4056.

e-book:
ISBN-13: 978-0-7880-2955-4
ISBN-10: 0-7880-2955-X

ISBN-13: 978-0-7880-2953-0
ISBN-10: 0-7880-2954-1   DIGITALLY PRINTED

This book is dedicated to my wife, Rachel, who has been my partner, my muse, my editor, my encourager, my taskmaster, my beacon of faith, and so much more for the last 35 years; without her, this book and the preceding two in this cycle would not have been possible. It is also dedicated to our children, Cameron and Andrew, who have helped spark the journeys I've taken through the lives of many people in this book by reminding me that who a person is today is not who they were in the past, nor who they will be in the future. I am blessed to have been entrusted with being a part of their journeys.

Finally, I must express my gratitude to David Runk, who was kind enough to approach me about writing the stories in the lectionary series in the first place; to Karyl Corson who has been patient with me throughout the process (including the time a cat tried to kill me — but that's another story); and to everyone at CSS Publishing who has been a part of these books. The confidence you have placed in me has been very much appreciated. I hope you have gotten what you were looking for.

Contents

First Sunday of Advent
Mark 13:24-37
The Wait — 13

Second Sunday of Advent
Mark 1:1-8
The Scout — 16

Third Sunday of Advent
John 1:6-8, 19-28
The One — 19

Fourth Sunday of Advent
Luke 1:26-38
What Child Is This? (Part 1) — 22

Nativity of the Lord
Luke 2:1-20
What Child Is This? (Part 2) — 25

First Sunday After Christmas
Luke 2:22-40
The Promise — 29

Second Sunday After Christmas
John 1:1-9,10-18
A Question For The Pastor — 33

Baptism of the Lord
Mark 1:4-11
Another Question For The Pastor — 36

Second Sunday after the Epiphany
John 1:43-51
The Recruit (Part 1) — 39

Third Sunday after the Epiphany
Mark 1:14-20
The Recruit (Part 2)   42

Fourth Sunday after the Epiphany
Mark 1:21-28
Mganga   44

Fifth Sunday after the Epiphany
Mark 1:29-39
Mission Creep   47

Transfiguration Sunday
Mark 9:2-9
A Moment Of Clarity   50

Ash Wednesday
Matthew 6:1-6, 16-21
The Gift   53

First Sunday in Lent
Mark 1:9-15
The Giver   56

Second Sunday in Lent
Mark 8:31-38
The Gift (Part 2)   59

Third Sunday in Lent
John 2:13-22
A Turn Of The Tables   62

Fourth Sunday in Lent
John 3:14-22
Here Comes The Judge   65

Fifth Sunday in Lent
John 12:20-33
The Appointed Hour   68

Liturgy of the Passion
Mark 14:1-15:47
Judas (Part 1)   71

Maundy Thursday
John 13:1-17, 31-35
Judas (Part 2)   74

Good Friday
John 18:1-19:42
A Final Rest   77

Resurrection of the Lord
John 20:1-18
Ghosts   80

Second Sunday of Easter
John 20
Ghosts (Part 2)   84

Third Sunday of Easter
Luke 24:36-48
Ghosts (Part 3)   87

Fourth Sunday of Easter
John 10:11-18
Listen   91

Fifth Sunday of Easter
John 15:1-8
Vines And Spines   95

Sixth Sunday of Easter
John 15:9-17
An Act Of Love   98

Ascension of the Lord
Luke 24:44-53
Anticipation   104

Seventh Sunday of Easter
John 17:6-19
Mysterious Ways 108

Day of Pentecost
John 15:26-27; 16:4b-15
The Draft, The Advocate, And Paul Hornung 112

Trinity Sunday
John 3:1-17
Table Talk 116

Proper 5 / Ordinary Time 10
Mark 3:20-35
What Family Is For 119

Proper 6 / Ordinary Time 11
Mark 4:26-34
Roots 122

Proper 7 / Ordinary Time 12
Matthew 4:35-41
The Eye Of The Storm 125

Proper 8 / Ordinary Time 13
Mark 5:21-43
Dead Girl, Live Girl 128

Proper 9 / Ordinary Time 14
Mark 6:1-13
Jesse From The Hood 131

Proper 10 / Ordinary Time 15
Mark 6:14-29
The Deal 134

Proper 11 / Ordinary Time 16
Mark 6:30-34, 53-56
Marathon Men 138

Proper 12 / Ordinary Time 17
John 6:1-21
Anything He Can Do...   141

Proper 13 / Ordinary Time 18
John 6:24-35
The Bread Of Life   144

Proper 14 / Ordinary Time 19
John 6:35, 41-51
Who Do You Think You Are?   147

Proper 15 / Ordinary Time 20
John 6:51-58
The Way To Life   150

Proper 16 / Ordinary Time 21
John 6:56-69
Tapping Out   153

Proper 17 / Ordinary Time 22
Mark 7:1-8, 14-15, 21-23
Garbage In, Garbage Out?   156

Proper 18 / Ordinary Time 23
Mark 7:24-37
A Matter Of Justice   159

Proper 19 / Ordinary Time 24
Mark 8:27-38
Declaration   163

Proper 20 / Ordinary Time 25
Mark 9:30-37
Declaration (Part 2)   166

Proper 21 / Ordinary Time 26
Mark 9:38-50
Loyal Opposition   169

Proper 22 / Ordinary Time 27
Mark 10:2-16
The New Pastor   171

Proper 23 / Ordinary Time 30
Mark 10:17-31
Rich Man's Burden   175

Proper 24 / Ordinary Time 31
Mark 10:35-45
Rich Man's Privilege   177

Proper 25 / Ordinary Time 32
Mark 10:46-52
The Darkness   181

Proper 26 / Ordinary Time 31
Mark 12:28-34
Teacher's Pet   184

All Saints' Day
John 11:32-44
The Promise   187

Proper 27 / Ordinary Time 32
Mark 12:38-44
The Widow   191

Proper 28 / Ordinary Time 33
Mark 13:1-8
Apocalypse   194

Reign of Christ / Proper 29 / Ordinary Time 34
John 18:33-37
The Truth   197

Thanksgiving Day
Matthew 6:25-33
What's For Dinner?   201

First Sunday of Advent

Mark 13:24-37

The Wait

Martin Schultz raised his head slightly and peered into the darkness. Even after a month of experience in the field, chasing after hostiles who never quite obliged by staying in one place long enough to catch, he could not believe how profoundly *dark* it was. *Like looking for a black cat at the bottom of a sack, at midnight,* he thought, and tried not to imagine what might be out there. "Why don't they just attack?" he muttered, surprising himself by saying it out loud.

"It's the magic," a voice said next to him.

He turned his head, made out a shape within the darkness: Dieter Holschbach, a veteran of almost a year on the plains. "What do you mean?"

"I mean it's the magic, Schultz. The hostiles believe the sun is their father — where they come from. If a warrior dies at night his soul has no place to return to, so they're condemned to walk the earth forever. That's why they never attack or fight at night, if they can avoid it."

There was a moment's pause, then a derisive laugh from Schultz's left. He turned toward the source: Sergeant Wayne, on the plains since before the war. "Why are you laughing, sergeant?"

"What Holschbach said — if I had a dollar for every time I've heard that old chestnut, I'd be back on Claremont Street in a house with a wife and kids, and nothing to worry about. Every recruit, every newspaper reporter fresh from out east — half the officers we get from the Point tell me that same thing, at some point. 'It's the magic,'" he repeated, and laughed again.

"If it's not the magic, what is it?" Holschbach asked defensively.

"When did you join up, Holschbach?"

"August, sergeant. August '67" His voice went up slightly at the end of his answer, almost as if he was questioning what he had said.

"Do you remember 'Pache Sam? He was the Indian scout over at the

Tenth, Company E, back at Fort Pennell?"

There was a hesitation in the dark, then an uncertain, "I think so. Was he the one who —" Holschbach's voice trailed off, leaving Schultz with a new unanswered question.

"That was him," the sergeant agreed. "I asked him, once why his people didn't attack at night — was it the magic, like everyone said? He laughed and said, 'Sergeant, we can't see in the dark any better than you can. You can't fight what you can't see.'"

"So it's not the magic?" Holschbach asked doubtfully.

"No — it's their eyes, same as us, 'cause they're people, just like us. People who happen to own something we want, so here we are."

There was a long silence in the dark, then, before Schultz cleared his throat softly and said, "Sergeant — so you don't believe in this war?"

There was an even longer silence, then, before Sergeant Wayne answered. "Son, that's a tall leap from what I just said. But I'll tell you what, I believe in the 21 dollars a month Uncle Sam pays me to do my job. The way I see it, a man would have to be getting at least captain's pay to actually believe in this God forsaken war."

Martin Schultz took that answer in and filed it somewhere where he could come back to it later and chew on it a bit. "Still," he muttered, "I wish they would just attack and get it over with."

"This is your first, right, Schultz? It *is* Schultz talking, right?" The sergeant said quietly in the dark.

"Yes, sir. Sergeant."

"Then let me give you a bit of advice you won't take. Don't be so anxious. There's no way anyone can tell you what it's really like, your first combat — you've heard a lot, probably read a lot — but no one can tell you what it's going to be like until you experience it yourself, least of all me or Holschbach. Truth is, out here on the plains, this kind of war, you almost never know when it's gonna happen — one minute everything's quiet, and then suddenly it's *there*, and you're fighting for your life. You're watching men die around you, and you're praying like the devil you won't be next. Tonight, we *think* it's going to happen tomorrow — and truth be told, you're kind of hoping it does, because you want to get it over with. But there's no way to know for sure. God's honest truth, the only thing you can be sure about is you can't be sure of nothin', except it'll be chaos on a scale you've never seen when it *does* happen."

"C'mon, Sergeant, you're scaring the boy," Holschbach responded, on his right.

"I'm not scared," Schultz said defensively.

"You should be," Sergeant Wayne said soberly. "Every battle, every skirmish, is like a judgment day out here — judging us, judging how ready we are. We should *all* be scared. Instead, we just tell the world to bring it on, because we can't imagine *not* making it through."

Martin Schultz peered out into the darkness for a bit, digesting what his sergeant had told him. After a time he said, "Can I be honest, Sergeant?"

"Please do, Schultz."

"If someone had told me all this back in Indiana, I wouldn't be here."

His sergeant laughed — a brief sound, quickly silenced. "And neither would I," he agreed almost immediately. "And yet, here we are. So we do what we need to do, Private Schultz. Eyes forward, keep watching for whatever it is that's coming — and pray you're ready."

In the darkness Martin Schultz nodded, and looked out into the night, waiting for an unknown tomorrow.

Second Sunday of Advent

Mark 1:1-8

The Scout

"Hey, Rev'rend, you 'wake yet? Somebody here to see you."

Jamison Lee opened his eyes, instantly awake... sort of. He lay still for a moment, one hand resting on the butt of a Colt Navy revolver, the other on the Bible that lay open on his chest. He blinked at the canvas above him and waited for the dream to fade. When the sights and sounds of battle were gone, he grunted, "What?"

Sensing it was now safe to poke his head in, a man stuck his head inside the tent and repeated, "Somebody here to see you."

Lee set the Bible aside and sat up on his cot, scratched his ribs beneath his undershirt, and stifled a yawn. "Somebody' who?"

The man shrugged. "You know I can't tell, Rev'rend. One of these is pretty much like the other, and I didn't ask his name."

Lee shook his head. "Rafe Logan, one of these is *not* pretty much like the other, any more than we are. We've had this discussion."

Logan grinned. "Have we, though? Or have I had it with some other preacher that looks just like you? It's why I don't call you missionaries by name — *you* all pretty much look alike to me, too."

"You're an idiot. Send him in." He stood up, sighed, scratched himself again and began to seriously consider whether he might have some kind of infestation. With water as scarce as it was, regular bathing was a luxury he hadn't enjoyed in a couple of months. The good thing, though, was that it was starting to affect his dreams — sometimes, now, he dreamt of water instead of battle.

That was a net win, as far as he was concerned.

He was contemplating that when the tent flaps parted and a man slipped inside. He was middle aged, stocky, with black hair that hung past his shoulders and the dark, slightly leathery complexion of the indians Lee had been ministering to since May. By his dress and other subtleties Lee could not lay a conscious hand on, the visitor looked like one of the local tribe, though he couldn't place the face. As he looked, he became aware that his visitor was studying him just as closely; he straightened up unconsciously, pulling his shoulders back. "How can I help you?" he asked, after a decent interval.

When the man answered, it was with slow deliberation, as though he was sorting through his vocabulary and finding the right English words. "I have come to find out why you are here. You have been talking to many people — talking, singing, telling stories not of our ancestors. Why?"

Lee nodded to show understanding. "I am a teacher, a storyteller, and my chief, you might call him — my chief has sent me here to share good news with your people."

The man looked at him closely. "Your chief — you mean President-Grant?" He said it as a hyphenated word.

"What? No, no — not the President. I mean God. The one who created the whole world, and who is the chief of all of us. *He* sent me."

The visitor nodded, then. "The Great Father."

Lee nodded in agreement. "Yes, the Great Father."

The visitor looked off into the distance, then back at Lee. "My people have many stories — *our* stories — of the Great Father, handed down to us by our ancestors. Why do you think you must come and tell us other stories? Some say it is not... right." He stepped across the tent in a couple of strides, causing Lee to tense, then wrapped a hand around Lee's wrist, lifted his arm and held Lee's hand alongside his own. "See, we are different. We do not need *your* stories. You do not need *ours*."

Lee gently detached his hand, said quietly, "We are not as different as you think. We believe that *all* men are the same, despite what you see when you look at them. We believe that the Great Father made *all* men the same, many years ago, and then they began to sin —" He hesitated when his visitors eyes narrowed, and he guessed what that meant. "They began to not listen to the Great Father, to not follow the ways he intended for them. They turned their backs on him — we call that sin."

The visitor nodded in cautious comprehension, then.

"And because of that, many years ago, God — the Great Father — sent his own son to try to reach out and convince men to turn back to him, to teach them his ways again. His son makes it possible for men to start listening and start living as his children again. To live all together, as one tribe — in peace."

There was a long pause, as the visitor looked at him appraisingly, then he grunted and asked, "Are you this man? The son?"

Lee smiled. "No — far from it. I'm just his messenger. I'm sort of a scout — I've come to see what is out here, and to tell your people about the son of the Great Father. The stories, the songs, everything I teach… it's all about him. I — we — want you to know about him, so that you can turn back to the Great Father, yourselves."

"Perhaps *we* never turned away. Perhaps we don't need this son."

Lee smiled again, and put an arm around his visitor's shoulder — but let go almost instantly, when the man tensed beneath the touch. "My friend, *everybody* needs the Great Father's son. Everybody needs Jesus. That's why I'm here, to tell you why you need him — and then to help you find him."

The visitor considered this, then said, "Perhaps *he* will find *us*."

"Well — I guess it's fair to say he will, but only if *you* are looking for *him*."

The visitor frowned. "This is very confusing. I am not sure it is right for my people to be hearing such confusing stories."

Lee sighed. "You're right — it is *very* confusing, but only because we started in the middle of the story. Pull up a stool, and let me start from the beginning, with the Great Father…" He waited until his guest had sat down, then sat down, himself, on the edge of the cot and picked up his Bible. "The way we heard the story from *our* ancestors," he said, "is that back in the very beginning, there was nothing but the Father… and his son —"

Third Sunday of Advent

John 1:6-8, 19-28

The One

The sky was starting to darken as they gathered up hymnals and packed them into the trunks for another week. A well-meaning gift from the Joliet Seminary Bible Society, the hymnals were a collection of Charles Wesley's greatest hits, painstakingly translated into the Menominee language by a pair of sisters. The girls' father had been among the first emissaries to the Menominee people. It was a labor of love, intended to help bridge the cultural divide between peoples.

It would have been a magnificent effort, if only the Menominee speakers had been Menominee *readers*, as well.

Still, Jamison Lee made them available every week, and every week they were largely ignored. Should the occasion arise he could, in good conscience, tell the Drummond sisters that their hymnals were brought out every week, for worship.

As they packed the last trunk, Two Bucks looked around to make sure they were alone, then caught Lee's eye and leaned toward him. "Can I ask you a question, Reverend Lee? In secret?"

Now what? Lee nodded. "Of course, you can ask me something in confidence."

Two Bucks looked around again, hesitated.

Lee took advantage of the moment to unscrew the cap from his canteen — a misappropriated relic of the war between the states — and raised it to his lips to take a swig of warm water.

"The Great Father's son — Jesus — you really *are* him, aren't you? You are just in secret."

It is to Jamison Lee's credit that the first two natural reactions — spluttering out the water and laughing out loud — came and went without even surfacing on his face as something he had to hold back. Instead he took a second drink — giving himself time to think — then carefully screwed the cap on and shook his head. "No. No, I am not," he said slowly. "But it is flattering to me that you think so." Pause. "I thought we settled this a couple of months ago."

"You told me you were not," Two Bucks confirmed. "But every day I watch you — I watch you teach and talk to us, and you make us hear his voice in you. So I thought, it must be you — you must be him. Just keeping it a secret now until you can test us. Your words have powerful magic, and you baptize us and tell us we are reborn. Those are signs of the Great Father's son."

Lee smiled. "Trust me, I am not him. I am not tricking you — I am not him."

"Then you must be one of the Great Father's special messengers — the ones you taught us about. A prophet — Issa, or Mosis, returned from the land of the dead to lead us," Two Bucks countered, eyeing him closely.

Lee's smile flickered. He reached out, put his hand on Two Bucks' shoulder. "I am not Jesus. I am not Isaiah or Moses, or *any* prophet. My life before this was —" He hesitated. "— not a godly one. I killed men, and ordered men to die, even sacrificed my own son on the altar of maintaining the union — and that does *not* make me Abraham," he added hastily.

Two Bucks just stared at him quizzically.

"Sorry — we haven't talked about that story, yet. But the point is, I've done bad things. I've drunk, played cards, cursed, and had lustful thoughts... I'm not a good man. I'm not a prophet of the Lord. But I *am* his instrument — or I've come to be, anyway."

He closed the lid on the trunk, latched it, and straightened up. "Two Bucks, for reasons I will never understand, God — the Great Father — saw fit to call me into his service after the war. I think he saved me — he gave me a purpose I'd been struggling to find, and that purpose was to share the good news of Jesus Christ with people who'd never heard that news before. So here I am. And here we are. I teach, and I share, and I hope that you understand me. But I'm just making way for Jesus — the real Jesus — to come into your lives. And when he does, he's going to turn your life upside down."

"What do you mean?"

"I mean I baptize you with water — but when Jesus comes along and becomes part of your life, he is going to bring you a spirit that will change your life forever. There's no going back when that happens. I hope you'll see that, some day."

There was a long silence, then Two Bucks said softly. "You say you are just a man — but could just a man lead another to this?" He reached out, picked up Lee's canteen and shook it; water sloshed within. He held it out toward Lee and said, "Can you baptize me with water, reverend — so that I can be ready for Jesus to come into my life?" He paused, lowered his voice even more, lowered his head. "I think I *need* him, reverend."

And when Jamison Lee took the canteen, he could have sworn there was a crackle in the air.

Fourth Sunday of Advent

Luke 1:26-38

What Child Is This? (Part 1)

Elizabeth Keane tried to steady her hand as she poured water into a cup but didn't succeed; it splashed on the hand holding the cup and she wiped it absentmindedly on her apron after she put down the pitcher and switched hands. She murmured, "This is some kind of awful mistake," then looked up quickly when she realized she had said it aloud.

Morgan Holloway reached across the kitchen table and patted her free hand.

She looked at him, then. "It *is*, right? A mistake? You make mistakes, don't you?"

Holloway smiled slightly. "Miss Keane — Elizabeth — I *do* make mistakes, but such is my profession that my mistakes generally get buried. *This*, though — in 32 years of practice, I've never been wrong. And I would hesitate to *ever* call the miracle of birth a mistake. Inconvenient, poorly timed, yes — but never a mistake. When the universe conspires to make a woman pregnant, and to bring a new life into the world, it's a blessing to celebrate, not a mistake to mourn. Ever."

"Well, there's always a first time, doctor." She planted her elbows on the table, put her head in her hands. "We never — well, only once, and it couldn't have been then. It's just impossible."

Holloway opened his bag, put away his stethoscope, and snapped it shut. "Be that as it may, Miss Keane, I would say in about five or six months, you are going to have fairly strong evidence to the contrary." He paused, drumming his fingers on the side of his bag for a moment or two, then asked bluntly, "Does the father know?"

Her expression hardened. "Considering *I* didn't know for sure until now, I don't expect that he would have any idea. He's gone — he's out west, bringing God to the heathens." There was an ironic twist to her mouth, then she shook her head. "I'm sorry. He's gone to live on the Lac des Morts Reservation, to do some mission work for the natives.

It wasn't the plan — we were going to get married — but then one of his old professors at the seminary asked him to go to Lac des Morts for a year. The professor was supposed to go, and then he became ill and needed time to recuperate — you get the idea. So Jamison went in his place. He said that's where he was being called, so that's where he needed to be, so…" She shrugged. "So *we* have to wait. And now *this*."

She put her head in her hands again, her brain whirling like a child's top. Morgan Holloway gave her a decent interval, then cleared his throat and said, "Not that you asked, but I will tell you you've got three options. One, you can do nothing — just stay here and let nature take its course, and be content to wear the scarlet letter — and for your child to forever be known as the out-of-wedlock Keane child, even if you do marry the father when he returns."

"We *are* getting married," she said firmly, suddenly aware of the chance that they might not. He might never come back, or he might come back and not believe the baby was his, or… she shook her head to banish the thoughts.

"Hear me out. I've known more than one young woman in your situation to move somewhere where no one knows them, and play the young widow. Women, especially childbearing women, are an asset, and nobody will look into your story too hard, if you can be half-convincing when you tell it."

"We *are* getting married," she repeated. "I see no need for me to pretend to be anything other than who I am."

He nodded. "Fine. Then that is your third option. Get a message to your husband-to-be now, and let him know what happened, so he can come back in time for you to get married, get pregnant, and have that child after an abnormally short gestation — no matter if it doesn't look premature, no one will say anything."

She shook her head. "You don't know him, doctor, but he's a stubborn man. He won't leave Lac des Morts until his time is up, and he has a replacement."

He nodded again. "I had a feeling you were going to say that, so the converse of that is for you to go to him. Go, find him, and tell him, then marry him and stay with him until he's ready to come home. A child should have a mother *and* a father — it's better for the child, and it's better for the mother. You've been blessed. Embrace it."

Elizabeth sighed. "I don't feel blessed, doctor."

"No doubt. And I know Reverend Roekle would frown on me drawing too close a parallel, here, but as I remember the story even Mary struggled when Gabriel told *her* she was pregnant. I don't doubt there was a great deal more back-and-forth discussion than we ever read in the good book, but she eventually did realize it was a blessing — and a duty, of sorts. Sort of her own calling, you might say — to bring a new life into the world."

"Do you really think so?" she asked quietly, her mind slowing, now, as a future started to form.

"As I heard the story, God created this entire world. I think the fact that he entrusted women with the task — the gift — of duplicating that feat on a smaller level, every time they give birth… it says something about the trust he has in you. I've said my piece — not that you asked," he repeated, with a sly smile, "and now I'll do the same thing God did. I'll trust you to make the decision."

There was another long pause, then Elizabeth Keane nodded to herself and sat up straight. "So, doctor — it seems I have a journey ahead of me, once my corn has been harvested. What will I need to know about traveling in my condition, when I'm another couple of months along?"

Morgan Holloway smiled, opened his bag and took out some paper and a pencil. "Let me make a list," he said, as he began to write.

Nativity of the Lord

Luke 2:1-20

What Child Is This? (Part 2)

The Indiana town where Martin Schultz had grown up sat at the southern tip of Lake Michigan, and the lake — in addition to providing commercial benefits — offered a moderating effect on the local climate, it tended to keep temperatures cooler in the summer and warmer in the winter. It was for that reason that he scarcely knew what to make of windchills in excess of twenty degrees below zero, as the wind finished its sprint across the northern plains and lashed the copse of evergreen trees where they had taken refuge. It was a razor sharp cold that had to be experienced to be understood… or believed.

And it was for *that* reason that he muttered a steady stream of invective as he stood next to a fire and tried to vanish into his buffalo skin coat. It was a passionate blend of English and German, learned at his grandfather's knee.

Around him, his comrades slept in tents that offered scant protection from the cold, though he fantasized that they lay warm and comfortable within their canvas wombs — and hated them for it. Fires burned throughout the small encampment, though they would be smoke and embers by morning. Around the perimeter of the camp and next to the horses, a handful of other sentries stood and stared out into the night, although everyone knew that no Indian in their right mind would be out and about on a night like this. They stood watch, because that's what such men did.

But that didn't mean they couldn't complain.

He was working his way back through Sergeant Wayne's family tree — you couldn't blame the weather, but you could blame the man who put you out in it — when he heard the snap of a twig to his left, then a rustle of branches almost too subtle to be heard above the wind. Trying not to expose any more of his skin than necessary, he turned toward the sound and raised his rifle, shouted a challenge into the bitter darkness.

And in the next moment, the cold became his *second* problem…

#

As shelters go, the wagon was better than nothing. But once the back wheel broke and immobilized it, Jamison Lee had worked frantically with an improvised shovel banking snow around three sides of it to make a decent windbreak for the lean-to canvas tent he improvised on the leeward side, with the wagon bonnet. A small fire burned just under the canopy, offering more light than heat.

As shelters go, the wagon was better than nothing — but not by much.

Beneath the canvas, in the little pocket of not-so-cold air, Elizabeth Keane (Elizabeth *Lee*, she reminded herself firmly) half-sat, half-lay against the wheel, seated on a wooden crate, covered with a couple of quilts. She hovered in a sort of dreamlike state, not fully believing where she was or what was happening to her — until a contraction hit, erasing any room for doubt. Dimly aware of Jamison's hand as she squeezed it, she would push until it seemed she might burst, then the sensation would ebb until next time.

And, God help her, the "next times" were coming closer together now.

"I should have left you at the boarding house," Jamison said, his voice apologetic. "I should never have agreed to bring you to the reservation until after the baby was born. And now…" He trailed off, unwilling to speak the truth he knew in his heart: this was no weather, these were no conditions, for a woman giving birth, or a newborn child. Despite anything he could do, there was no way for this to end well. It had been a fool's errand to bring her out here, and now they would pay the price for his stupidity.

He dabbed her face with a rag, wiped away sweat, and wished he could wipe away time — take them back to town, and safety. She squeezed his hand again, looked at him out of the corner of her eye and flashed a ghost of a smile. "I didn't give you a lot of choice, Colonel. I can be kind of stubborn, if you hadn't noticed."

He raised her hand with his, kissed it tenderly. "No, I never noticed."

"Liar," she said softly, and closed her eyes, tried to breathe normally. After some timeless interval she opened her eyes wide. "There's someone out there," she said breathlessly, turned her face so she could look at him directly. "There's someone out there," she repeated, louder this time.

He was about to say something about her imagination when he heard the horses whinny nervously. Then, over the noise of the wind, he heard boots in the snow, and voices — and the crunchy rolling noise of wagon wheels. A few shouted commands, then a head poked into the tent tentatively. The face was pink with cold, beneath a fur hat, and bore a thick brush of a mustache that was solidly frozen. "Are you folks in need of assistance?" the man asked after a quick size-up of the scene. Without waiting for an answer, the man went on, "My name is Sergeant Wayne — Eustice Wayne. We've come to help, if you need it."

Jamison would have laughed, if he hadn't felt like crying. "Brother, you have no idea!" he said, standing in a crouch and extending his hand to the newcomer. He was about to say more when his wife began to groan again, and he turned back to her.

Eustice Wayne watched for a moment or two, then pulled his head out and shouted over his shoulder, "Schultz! Get the surgeon in here!"

#

It was the sort of daybreak that belonged in a painting — an achingly bright sun spilling its light on a blanket of dazzling snow, while crystals of ice drifted on the air like tiny, microscopic diamonds. In the back of one of the supply wagons, cocooned in buffalo robes, Elizabeth and Jane Lee slept deeply even as the wagon jolted along what passed for a trail. Jamison Lee and Eustice Wayne sat on opposite sides of the wagon, talking quietly so as not to disturb mother or child — if that would have been possible.

"Okay," Jamison said wearily, "I understand what you're saying, but it's still a miracle in my book that you were transporting the post surgeon to Fort Bellah. If he hadn't been there — if *you* hadn't been there…"

Wayne grunted. "In my experience, it's best not to focus on the coulda-beens, Reverend Lee. Just be thankful we were nearby, with a surgeon, and let it go at that."

"But I don't get that, either. Don't get me wrong — but you shouldn't have been out on a night like that."

The sergeant grudged a smile. "Believe me, reverend, my men and I were thinking the same thing — right up until we saw your fire. Then we knew why we were there."

"Can you tell *me*, then?"

Wayne considered this for a while, sitting in silence as the wheels crunched through the snow, finally shook his head. "I don't rightly think I can, reverend. All I can tell you is what I know. The boys and me were bivouacked for the night, just starting to go to sleep, when this stranger walks up to one of my pickets and says he has something to tell us. Told him that there was a family — a man and a woman — broke down on the road to Lac des Morts, and the woman was fixin' to have a baby. And they needed our help." He paused.

Jamison waited a moment, then nodded. "Go on."

"Well, that was a pretty outlandish story, on a night like that, so my sentry was going to just take this stranger prisoner for the night, so's I could talk to him in the morning. And that's when a whole bunch more of 'em stepped out of the woods and just stood there. It was dark, of course, so he couldn't see how many — but there was a bunch of them. And before he could say or do anything else, they just turned and walked away — faded into the darkness." Wayne shook his head. "Damnedest thing I ever heard. If another couple pickets hadn't seen the same thing, I wouldn't have believed him — but they did." He shrugged. "That's the story, reverend, take it or leave it. We figure they were indians, maybe a hunting party that saw you."

Jamison nodded. "That's the only thing that makes sense, isn't it? What did they look like — or did *he* look like, the first one?"

There was another, longer silence. "Well, now — that's the really interesting part, reverend. When I asked him, Schultz couldn't rightly say, nor could any of the others. They were just there — and gone. But if they weren't indians, who were they?"

It was a question that would linger — but not for *too* long. In the end, some miracles exist to be appreciated, not explained.

First Sunday After Christmas

Luke 2:22-40

The Promise

The parlor smelled of lavender and starched white linen. Jamison Lee pulled out his watch, checked the time — about two minutes later than the *last* time he checked — and put it back into his pocket. His fingers played unconsciously with the fob; he looked across the room, where Elizabeth and the baby sat on a red velvet settee, caught her eye and smiled. She smiled back then went back to fussing with the baby's gown. Somewhere, a clock ticked loudly, though he needed no reminder of the time passing: the slowly coiling spring that seemed to have taken up residence in his chest was doing a fine job of that.

When he couldn't stay silent any longer, he cleared his throat and said softly, "Libby, it's a quarter of ten. Shouldn't we be leaving?"

Without looking at him, she shook her head slightly; when she did raise her eyes to him, her expression was blithely unconcerned. "Don't be silly, Colonel — my grandparents helped *build* Saint Michael's. They wouldn't dare start a service without my grandmother being there. Particularly not such a momentous one." As if to punctuate that last statement, she bowed her head toward the baby and made a face; the baby grinned and cooed.

"There you are," a soprano voice said suddenly, as though in response to the question. Jamison stood up as Grandmother Keane swept into the parlor. She was tall but frail, and the thought crossed Jamison's mind that she looked as though a good, stiff wind might just pick her up and carry her away — only her natural expression seemed to say, "It wouldn't dare." She was wearing a dress that would have been appropriate for being received by the Queen of England; failing that, it would do for a church service. She glanced at Jamison, then turned her full attention to Elizabeth and the baby. "And this would be —?" she asked.

Elizabeth stood up, then, turning to show the child to her. "Grandmother Keane, I would like you to meet Jane Gretchen Lee —

your great granddaughter." To the baby, she raised her tone and said, "Say hello to Great Grandmother, Jane. Say hello."

One carefully shaped eyebrow arched. "*Jane* Gretchen? Elizabeth, you know perfectly well that it is the tradition in the Keane family to name the first girl after the child's grandmother and great-grandmother, just as your sister was, and your mother before her, rest their souls."

Elizabeth hesitated, glanced at Jamison who stood silently by, idly wishing he were somewhere else. Anywhere else. She looked at her grandmother, then, and said, "Yes, of course. But it turns out that Jamison's family has a tradition as well, that the first son and first daughter bear the names of their grandparents. When Jamison told me that, I thought it was only right to use his mother's name, and then yours. You have been like a mother to me, all these years."

Grandmother Keane sniffed, cast another glance at Jamison. "I suppose your mother was pleased, at least."

He shrugged. "Possibly, Grandmother Keane. It's hard to know, her being dead and all." He smiled slightly, to dull the edge.

It didn't help. There was an icy moment of silence, then a brisk, "I see." She turned back to Elizabeth. "Well, there's nothing to be done about it now, I suppose. I will have a word with Reverend Bixby before the service, to let him know." She sniffed again, then addressed Jamison without turning to him. "Will the rest of your family be joining us at the church? I was given to understand that you have a son."

Jamison caught his breath, about to respond sharply, but just shook his head. "No, ma'am. My son was killed in the War, at a place called White's Run, and I have no other family." He looked at his wife and daughter, then, and smiled. "Just the two most beautiful women in the world."

"I see. Perhaps you would do us the honor of going 'round front and making sure our carriage is ready?"

"Be glad to," he said honestly, and left after a quick, formal bow to Grandmother Keane.

When he was gone from the parlor, Grandmother Keane stared after him and said, "I'm sorry if I insulted him or brought up bad memories. But I've been looking forward to this day for so long — so many years of waiting."

Elizabeth cocked her head slightly. "Years? I didn't even know until last summer."

"I —" She hesitated, looked around, lowered her voice. "I never told you, Elizabeth, but I suppose I should, now. A long time ago — well, after your mother died, when you were born — I was distraught. I was caught in grief for a long time, I didn't understand how or why such a thing would happen. Of course, we had *you*, our granddaughter, but had lost your mother. Whatever joy you brought seemed… hollow. Do you understand?"

Elizabeth nodded, trying to process what she was hearing.

"And then, one day, when you were just turned a year old, I had a dream. Well, it must have been a dream. I woke up here — I had fallen asleep in the parlor, after lunch — and the nurse had taken you to your room, your grandfather was at work, so I slept. And when I woke up, a man I didn't know was standing here. He was standing right where you are, in fact. And he just looked at me with these kind, compassionate eyes and said, 'You're sad, aren't you?'"

She paused, and her eyes seemed to be fixed on the memory she was dredging up. "I said of course I was. And then he reached out and touched my hand, and I was suddenly filled with this warm feeling as he said, 'Gretchen, I promise you, one day you will have a great granddaughter, and she will grow to do wonderful, marvelous things… and her name will be Madeline.'" Her eyes changed focus back to the present, then, and she said, "After your mother, my daughter."

"Of course," Elizabeth said softly.

"And he didn't tell me anything more — just that I would live to see her born. And so I waited years… and years. When you wrote that you had finally married, I was so excited for you, and for me… and then he died, and I nearly lost hope. More years went on, and you didn't remarry, and I thought it would never happen. And then, just like a miracle, I got your telegram about the child. Imagine my surprise — I didn't even know you had married again."

Elizabeth felt her face flush. "Yes, I suppose it was a surprise. I'm sorry."

"Don't be sorry, dear. It was a joyful surprise. But the best part of all was that now I knew the promise had been kept. And then…" She made a helpless gesture. "So, there will be no Madeline to carry on the tradition, and the promise is *not* true."

She was about to continue when Jamison returned. He looked at Elizabeth, then at Grandmother Keane, trying to gauge whether he was interrupting something important. After a moment or two he gave up and just said, "The carriage is ready."

"Then we should be on our way," Grandmother Keane said briskly. "We shan't be late for church, or Reverend Bixby will never let me hear the end of it." She bustled out of the room, leaving her granddaughter and grandson-in-law staring after her.

A moment of silence passed between them, then Jamison shook his head and ushered his wife and daughter to the door with a motion of his hand. As they passed, Elizabeth said, "How do you feel about the name 'Madeline?'"

Jamison started to respond, then stopped, started again, with a puzzled expression. "This isn't a theoretical question, is it?" he said to the back of her head. And when she didn't answer, he sighed.

Second Sunday After Christmas

John 1:1-9,10-18

A Question For The Pastor

There was a knock at the door, and a diffident, "Pastor?"

Puzzled, Jamison Lee looked up from his reading, raised an eyebrow, and beckoned for his caller to come in. She was tall for ten, with scuffed elbows and knees to testify that her mother's efforts to curb her tomboy activities had not yet borne fruit. "'Pastor?' Not 'Papa?'" he wondered.

She shrugged, her expression serious as she sat down on the chair across from him, her feet easily touching the floor, even as the chair threatened to swallow her. "It's more of a 'pastor' question than a 'Papa' question. Mrs. Sievert said I should ask you."

"Ah. I'll have to thank her." He put a bookmark in his book and set it aside, folded his hands on his desk and gave her his full attention. "So what can I do for you, Jane? This is about Sunday school, I assume?"

"It is," she confirmed. "We were reading the Gospel from John 1, and I suddenly wondered why God sent John like that. I mean, if Jesus is all powerful and can do anything, why not just send Jesus? Wouldn't that have been a lot easier?"

"Oh, probably — but I don't think it's quite that simple. For one thing, people have to *choose* to accept Jesus as their Savior. Being powerful doesn't mean he can *make* them do it."

"Why not?"

"Well, it —" He hesitated, turned over several answers in his mind, than just said, "It doesn't work that way. God gives us the ability to make choices, for right or wrong. A long time ago, people chose wrong — now he's giving them a chance to choose right, again. But it has to be a choice. Do you remember the Lac des Morts Reservation — you were pretty young when we left, not even three, I guess. But I went there, kind of like John, to pave the way for another pastor who would come along behind me and build a proper church. But to make *his* work possible, I had to prepare the way by talking about Jesus, God, sin, and forgiveness, so that people can make the right choice."

"I don't remember the reservation," his daughter said, shaking her head. "But I remember you and Mom talking about it. It was hard work, wasn't it?"

"Very hard work," he agreed. "But necessary. You know how you help Mom in the garden? What do you do every spring, before a seed ever goes in the ground?"

Her features changed as she thought about the question, answered it slowly as things came to her. "We clean it out, we take out the stuff that lay in the garden over winter. We weed, if there's anything there. We dig up the ground. We —"

"So there's a lot that goes into it. What do you think would happen if you and Mom didn't do all that — just went out one day and threw seeds on the ground?"

"We wouldn't get too many vegetables, I guess."

"Right — because to have the best chance of thriving, they need all that preliminary work done. Just like Jesus, to give the people the best choice of hearing and understanding who he is — and the best chance of accepting him as their Savior — needed someone to do preparation before he arrived. That was John. And, like I said, me at Lac des Morts. I prepared the way, so Reverend Seward could come in and have something to build on. Does that make sense?"

She nodded. "I think so."

"The thing to remember is that *everything* we do, if we're doing it for God, is important. Even if we might not see how it helps right away, it's going to make a difference down the line — somehow, somewhere." He unfolded his hands, sat back in his chair. "Now, next week you can tell Mrs. Sievert you've had your question answered."

"Maybe. She said she was thinking about not being there next week."

"Oh? Why is that?"

"Something about getting too old. She was looking really tired after class, today."

Jamison smiled, and nodded a little. "I see. Well, I will talk to her and see if there's anything I can do to help."

Madeline Lee got up from the chair and half-skipped to the door, paused as she was leaving the office and looked back at him. "Oh — one other question: why do you always call me Jane, unless I'm in trouble? My name is Madeline."

"It is," he agreed, "but it wasn't always."

She looked at him, tilted her head to one side.

"It's a long story," he answered. "Ask your mother."

Baptism of the Lord

Mark 1:4-11

Another Question For The Pastor

There was a knock at the door, and a hesitant, "Pastor?"

Puzzled, Jamison Lee looked up from his reading and raised an eyebrow, beckoned for his caller to come in. She was tall and slender, wearing a freshly starched gray skirt that went down nearly to her ankles, and a white blouse with modest frills and sleeves that buttoned tightly around her wrists. In her right hand, she held a folded newspaper. "'Pastor?' Not 'Papa?'" he wondered aloud, mindful that he was echoing the past.

She shrugged, let a faint smile flash across her face as she sat down on the chair across the desk from him. By long habit, she sat up straight and did not slouch against it. "I think it's more of a 'pastor' question than a 'Papa' question — for now," she said diffidently.

He turned his book over on his desk, leaned forward and rested his arms on the desk. "Go ahead, Jane."

"The Gospel lesson today — about Jesus getting baptized, and the Holy Spirit descending on him like a dove. Do you think it really happens that way — to regular people, I mean? I know there's several gospels that tell it the same way, for Jesus. Does it just come like that — boom, it's there?"

Jamison nodded. "The synoptics tell pretty much the same story, John has a little different version. Everybody seems to agree that the Holy Spirit descends upon Jesus, and that's when he really seems to find his sense of who he is, and what he's supposed to do — his sense of mission. Is that what you mean?"

"Yes — does it happen to regular people that way, too, all of a sudden?"

Jamison leaned back in his chair, then, and folded his arms over his chest while he considered the question. After a bit he nodded and said, "Sometimes. I think I can say sometimes it does."

Baptism of the Lord

"Is that how it happened for you — I mean, when you decided to become a pastor, was it a moment like that?" She looked at him closely.

He smiled. "Not exactly. I think the Lord was chasing me for a while, before I finally let him catch up with me. There were a thousand little things — I was trying to sort through what had happened in the War. But then, yes, I guess it was sort of sudden, at that. I think I was led to that point, to get me ready — and then had a moment of sudden understanding. That would have been the moment the Holy Spirit landed on my shoulder, told me I was supposed to be a pastor. Why do you ask?"

It was her turn for silence and for several heartbeats father and daughter just looked at one another across the desk. Finally, she said, "I think I had that moment, today, after church — when I was cleaning up. I saw a newspaper, and then all of a sudden it hit me like a thunderbolt — I knew what I had to do." She smiled shyly. "What *God* wants me to do."

Jamison leaned forward again, tried to look encouraging when every fiber of his being urged caution. *This can't be going to a good place,* he thought. Aloud, he said, "I think that's wonderful, Jane. But I thought you already knew — you're going to be a teacher."

She took a deep breath. "You read about what happened over in South Dakota, last week? The battle with the indians?"

He nodded. "At Wounded Knee, yes, with the Sioux. It was a horrible thing. The papers are trying to paint it as a battle, but —" He hesitated. "I've got my doubts. Everything I've read, everything I've heard, makes me think it was something darker. I know how mistakes can happen — and how they can become disasters. I have a feeling something like that happened." He shook his head. "It's a tragedy, for certain. I'm afraid we've done horrible things in the name of progress — uprooting people from their homes, penning them up when they used to be free."

She nodded, then. "All these years of hearing you talk about what it was like at the Lac des Morts Reservation made me think you might feel that way. And I'm glad."

Jamison felt a prickly feeling along his spine, and for a moment he couldn't quite catch his breath. "Oh?"

"Well — now that I've finished normal school, I think I'm supposed to go to Lac des Morts to teach on the reservation. And if they don't need me there, I'll find another reservation that *does* need a teacher — but that's what I'm going to do. It's what came to me today. I need to reach out and help those people."

"I thought you were going to go to Milwaukee? You have a friend, there —"

"There are children on the reservation who need me, Father. I am certain of that. They can never be part of this country if we don't make the effort to educate them — and not just in *our* ways, either — we need to help them learn their own ways, so they won't be lost. We've taken so much — I think we owe them something, at least."

"When we left, there was no school. There wasn't even a permanent church."

She smiled. "It's been seventeen years, Father. I hope they have remedied that situation. But if not — then all the more reason they need me."

There was a very long silence, then. "Are you absolutely certain this is what you want to do?" Jamison asked finally. "It will be a hard life, whether it's at Lac des Morts or somewhere else. Life on the reservation is no life for a young woman."

"Mother lived there for three years."

"She wasn't alone."

"I won't be, either. Don't you tell us that God is always with us? And if the Holy Spirit is going to take me here, it's not going to leave me on my own, is it?"

Her father grunted. "No, I don't suppose it will." He paused, drummed his fingers, then sighed and said, "There's just one thing — if you're going to do this, *you* have to tell your mother."

His daughter looked at the floor for a moment, then looked up. "I already have. And she said the same thing about telling *you*."

Father and daughter smiled at one another, then — and Jamison had the uncanny feeling that the Holy Spirit was smiling, too.

Second Sunday after the Epiphany

John 1:43-51

The Recruit (Part 1)

"My brother tells me you've been trying to recruit him."

Mark Randall picked up the rag with which he had been wiping down the bar, shook it out gently and refolded it, began to wipe again. "Am I being successful?" he asked, without looking up at first — and then he looked directly into the eyes of the man who had spoken. "Is he coming with me?"

"You mean, is he going to put his life on hold, so he can join you on some hare-brained trip to Africa?" The man frowned. "Yes, it seems like he is. He's got his mind set, and I don't think I can change it."

Randall grinned. "'Hare-brained,' huh? I haven't heard it called that before. Except by my sister, maybe. What's so hare-brained about wanting to help people?"

"Nothing — except these are people in a war zone. This place you're going to —"

"Kufasi," Randall interjected.

"Kufasi. *Time Magazine* says they're in the middle of a civil war, and they're like the third most dangerous country for foreigners to go to in Africa. And I'm not sure they even *want* your help. Barry tells me you haven't even been invited by the Kufasan government — you're just going."

Randall nodded. "That's right. The church I go to, here, has been in touch with some of the NGOs over there, and they found out there's a former mission station at a village called M'Batha. The people in that province are having a pretty bad time of it, so our plan is to open the mission again. We'll be helping people, sharing the gospel, and making a difference. Your brother is an agronomist, and that's going to be huge for them. We've also got a civil engineer, some teachers, a nurse…" He ticked them off on his fingers, then paused and appeared to be thinking. "In fact, the only thing we *don't* have, yet, that I think would be really useful is a doctor — *Doctor* Brown."

Tom Brown laughed. "You're not suggesting that *I* go, are you? Because if you are, you're crazier than I thought you were. I've got a nice practice going right now — there's absolutely no reason for me to walk away from that."

"Even for a year?"

"Even for a day. You may not get this, but I've got responsibilities."

Randall nodded again, began wiping slowly. "Of course. Those school physicals aren't going to give themselves, are they?" With his head down, he rolled his eyes so he could look at the man across from him. "Barry told me a lot of what you're doing these days is school physicals, and immunizations."

"Someone has to. It may not be up to your standards of social importance, but what I do matters, no matter what you might think."

"No doubt, no doubt — I didn't mean any harm. I know there's a lot of good, solid, everyday medicine that has to happen, not everybody gets the chance to be Trapper John. But did you ever watch a kid die from dysentery? No, because it doesn't happen here. My dad saw it, in his days down in Latin America. And it happens in Kufasi. The simplest things can have the most profound impact — you know that. In a city where there's a thousand doctors, your practice is important — but in a village where there's only one, it would be life changing. And you *want* to make a difference."

Tom Brown frowned. "You think you know me?"

"I know who you wanted to be, ten years ago. You wanted to be a healer, making lives better, making people healthier. You wanted to come to people in crisis and show them a way through. You wanted to make a better world. And I think you will, regardless — but I also know you can make the most difference in a place like Kufasi. Even if it's just for a year — how many lives could you save? How many souls could you touch?" He picked up the rag, refolded it, set it aside. "I think — no, I *know* — you've got a comfortable life and a comfortable practice... but I think you *want* a calling. Come with me — with us — and we can make that happen. We can change their world, show them what the love of Christ is all about. Are you in?"

After a bit, the other man shook his head ruefully and said, "What did you do before you tended bar? Sell cars?"

Mark smiled. "So that's a yes?"

"You seem to know me pretty well — what do you think?"

"I think you had better make sure your passport is up to date."

Third Sunday after the Epiphany

Mark 1:14-20

The Recruit (Part 2)

Tom Brown mopped his face with a damp handkerchief, stuffed it in his pocket and took another swig of water from his water bottle. Next to him, Mark Randall cleared his throat. Tom looked at him and said seriously, "I swear, if you say 'it's not the heat, it's the humidity' again, I will kill you in your sleep."

The statement caused one of the three young men working on their Toyota land cruiser to look up sharply — then, after assessing the situation, he went back to tinkering with the engine and said something quietly to his companions. They all looked at the foreigners and laughed. Mark noted this, and said, "You speak English? Sir — with the socket wrench — you speak English, right?"

The young man finished tightening the bolt he had been working on and set the wrench aside, nodded. "Yes, sir. My father taught me." He made an expansive gesture with one hand. "The owner of the garage you talked to, this morning."

"Right. He spoke very well. And so do you. What is your name?"

"Alemayehu — you can say Albert."

Mark stepped toward him, extended his hand. "Albert, my name is Mark. I'm pleased to meet you."

Albert wiped the grease from his own hand, then shook hands with a slightly bemused expression. "Pleased to meet you," he echoed.

Mark gestured toward the land cruiser. "I couldn't help but notice that you really seem to know your way around a diesel engine. Have you been doing this long?"

The young man smiled shyly. "Only since I was old enough to look under the hood. My father taught me as soon as I could hold a spanner. I work on cars, trucks, motors of all kind. I have learned much."

"I can see that. If you don't mind my saying so, we could really use you, where we're going."

Third Sunday after the Epiphany

The young man's eyebrows drew together. "What do you mean?"

"My friends and I, we're going to a village called M'Batha, about a hundred and thirty miles from here. There is a mission station there that we're going to reopen. There will be a doctor, some nurses, a school, a church — and I'm sure we're going to need a good mechanic like you. If you come with us, you can help people — help us teach them about Jesus. You know Jesus, don't you?"

Another shy smile. "Not personally — but my father taught us the Bible stories." He paused. "I have my job here, sir."

"I understand. Here you fix cars. And trucks. And I can see that you're very good at your job. But if you come with us to M'Batha, you can help us to fix hearts and souls, as well."

When Albert didn't answer at once, Tom Brown mopped his face again and said, "You may as well say 'yes' now, Albert — my friend doesn't take 'no' for an answer."

Albert looked at both men uncertainly. "Why are you doing this?"

Mark shrugged. "I believe I have been called to it. I don't know why, but this is what God has been preparing me for all my life. So here I am. My friend — Doctor Brown, here — is here because he wants to make a difference in people's lives. That's why we're all here, in the end."

Albert realized his companions had stopped working and were watching them. He said something short, and both men shrugged and went back to what they were doing. He looked back at Mark, then. "So you want me to be a — a —" he hesitated, found the word, "a missionary?"

"Well — in a word, yes. A missionary within your own country, to your own people. But yes. We need your help — and so do the people around M'Batha."

There was another long pause, then the young man shrugged. "If I can help you to fix hearts and souls, then yes, I will go with you. But I have to tell my father."

Mark smiled. "Tell you what, Albert — you finish this car, and we'll go tell him together. We've got a long road ahead of us."

Fourth Sunday after the Epiphany

Mark 1:21-28

Mganga

"You taunt forces you do not understand, and you teach lies to my people. There is no place for you here," Albert said, his expression strained as he formed the words.

Mark Randall and Tom Brown didn't notice; they were intent on the other man in the room — tall, thin, wearing a faded white *kanzu*, the loose fitting, ankle-length tunic that most of the local men wore. His skin was weathered, and his hair was short and white. He glared back at them, absently fingering a hide bag hanging from a cord around his neck, beneath his *kanzu*. After Albert had been silent for a few moments, he added another brief sentence, waited.

"You should leave. You should all leave," the mechanic translated, and made a helpless gesture that said, *I'm sorry*.

"Please tell Mister Djimon that we appreciate his suggestion, but we are confused," Mark answered. "We do not lie, and we do not taunt anyone. We are here to help the people of M'Batha. We care about them, just as he does."

Translated, that set off a torrent of words in response. He stopped for breath a couple of times, during which Albert started to translate, but then started talking again, overriding the voice of the translator. Eventually he stopped abruptly, looked at Albert expectantly; the young man began to speak. "He says you tell lies about a white man's God that has no place here. He is a —" he struggled, then grasped the word, "— a European colonial God, with no power. The power here is in the earth, and the trees, and the —" he struggled again, then shrugged. "— It's kind of like *souls* of the animals, but not exactly. Spirit, maybe. It's the thing that animates them and gives them life."

"Okay. Spirit works, I guess."

"And the healer — the doctor — he knows nothing about how nature balances nature in our world. He speaks of children's stories, where tiny little warriors can enter a body and make it sick, when everyone knows it is the presence of dark spirits at war with the light that causes imbalance and sickness in the body." He added, "He said," almost as an afterthought.

"Seriously? Are we back in the Dark Ages?" It was the first thing the doctor said since the old African gentleman began to speak.

Mark made a slight motion with his hand, to urge quiet.

The doctor gestured back dismissively. "No — I want to know what's going on here. It's hard enough trying to do frontier medicine, here — why is he trying to make my life that much harder?"

Albert did not translate the question for their visitor, instead explained, "Doctor Tom, he is *mganga* —" The young man hesitated again, searching his vocabulary. "— like a, what do you call — a 'witch doctor.'"

At that, Mark had a sudden flash of the old Alvin and the Chipmunks record —

Ooo eee, Ooo ah ah, ting tang
Walla walla, bing bang

— and almost laughed. Instead, he sighed and said, "How serious is he? Is he going to be a problem?"

"More than he already has?" Tom Brown added. "I just got that boy stabilized on Diazepam for his seizures — I don't want the witch doctor here, talking Mom into not giving him his medicine."

"I know," Mark answered.

"And I don't want him hanging around outside the clinic, harassing people when they come in. We're trying to help these people, I don't know what *he's* trying to do."

Albert, who had watched their conversation, licked his lips and said diffidently, "Doctor Tom — I ask you to believe that Djimon is trying to help his people, as well. He is a practitioner of the old ways, and his beliefs are old, but he holds them as dearly as you do." When both missionaries looked at him in surprise, he flushed. "I am sorry — I know I should just translate, but —"

"No, no, no," Mark said quickly. "We need you to tell us what you know, when things like this come up." He glanced at Tom. "We just didn't realize that the old ways were as strong as they are here."

"It's damn near like living in the Dark Ages," the doctor muttered.

Mark started to answer, then stopped, and looked thoughtful. "Maybe," he said. "On the other hand, how many people do you know, back home, who look at their horoscope first thing, when they open a newspaper in the morning? It's hard for people to give up the things they think they know — that give order to their world."

"Tell me you're not taking *his* side," the doctor said.

"No. We know the truth — the real truth. But we're not going to make friends and influence people by coming in and telling them we know better than they do. We have to figure out how to work with them, or nothing's going to come of this."

"But —"

"You're a doctor, Tom — you're used to knowing more than everyone else, and to people *knowing* you know. But here — it's a different story. I think they've had enough people come in and try to tell them what to think, already." He looked at their mechanic, then. "Albert — tell Djimon that we understand what he's saying. We are not trying to tell them what to think — but we have learned some important things about how to keep people from suffering. We're here to show them those things."

Albert relayed the message to Djimon, who took a few moments to digest, then answered in a slightly-less-angry tone. Albert repeated it back in English. "He says that he will not stand by while your ways take the spirit of his people — but he is willing to listen if you will explain, if you truly know what you are talking about."

Mark smiled, then, and relaxed for the first time since the conversation started. "Please tell him we do, and we will be happy to explain."

Fifth Sunday after the Epiphany

Mark 1:29-39

Mission Creep

"That's it," Tom Brown said wearily, and sat down next to Mark Randall, took the glass of water that he offered. "We have officially vaccinated every child in this village against smallpox — and Albert tells me there were a few people from one of the nearby villages as well. It has also been nine weeks since Chuma had a seizure, so Mom must be keeping him on his meds, despite Djimon. Which reminds me — we're going to need more Diazepam. And a bunch more antibiotics, and I'd like to see what we can do about TB —"

Mark smiled. "You know the drill, Tom. Write it up, we'll let the church back home know, and if there's anything you think is critical, we'll see what we can scavenge back in Mji'na Bahari."

"Good God, Mark, *everything* is critical. A simple infection here is a life and death battle, and we've seen it a dozen times. Djimon may be in love with the good old days, but his herbs and chants don't do a thing against a case of cellulitis. But I told you the big thing a month ago — what we really need is half a dozen more nurses, so we can start a traveling clinic. Think you could drop a line to God, and see what he can do?"

"I'll put it on my list. But that brings up something I wanted to talk about: we *are* getting a few new people flying into Mji'na Bahari next week, but they're not nurses."

"But that's what we need."

"Yes — *but*. We're doing a lot of great things, here — no question. And we definitely need to *maintain* the medical program as it is, but I think with all the success you and the nurses have been having, it's time for us to shift the focus a little bit. We've been showing these people what modern medicine can do — but we haven't spent a lot of time on the mission part of why we're here — the gospel mission. We've been very focused on the medical mission, but I'm afraid we've let the gospel mission slide, and it's time we fixed that. We've proven we're here to help, they should be willing to listen to us."

"Isn't that just going to be borrowing trouble from Djimon? He already things we're trying to snatch the old ways away from his people — you know, voodoo, witchcraft, hexes — all that stuff from the good old days."

"I think you're mixing up a couple of different belief systems, there, but you're right — he is very insistent that *his* people should keep to the old ways. But I think that may have less to do with theological principles than maintaining his grip on them."

The doctor considered this, nodded after just a beat or two. "I'm sure you're right — no matter what he's convinced himself of, I'm sure it comes down to power. Which is all the more reason not to tick him off, no?"

"Well — it's gonna happen sometime, so we may as well rip the bandage off now. In all seriousness, we *are* here to teach these people about Jesus Christ, Tom — you've seen, you *know* how steeped in superstition they are. We can help show them the truth, show them where the love and caring that you and your people are sharing with them comes from."

The doctor sighed. "I still like the idea of a traveling clinic."

"So do I — but what good does it do if we care for their bodies, but not their souls?"

Tom Brown grunted. "None, I suppose."

"We're not here to jam it down anybody's throat, Tom — you know that. But we want to share the gospel, the good news, with them — and that's going to take some resources."

"I suppose," the doctor said, with less conviction than the words implied.

"The way I see it, we want you along when we go out into the surrounding villages — we just want you to be the dessert, and not the main course."

"Dessert it is," the doctor agreed, and stood up. "But I still need to order a bunch of supplies, and maybe make a buying trip to Mji'na Bahari, even if we are just an afterthought."

Mark stood up, as well. "Never an afterthought," he promised his friend. "Just not what we want to focus on right now. It's time for us to bring the word of God to these people."

Tom snorted. "Right. Give my regards to Djimon."

Transfiguration Sunday

Mark 9:2-9

A Moment Of Clarity

There are certain deficiencies in language that don't become evident until they are ruthlessly exposed by events in the real world. There is the English word "rain," for instance, which is generally defined as water condensed from the air, falling in drops. In Swahili, the word is *mvua*, which translates literally as "drops of water falling from the clouds."

Neither definition takes into account the experience of a tropical rainstorm in the uplands of Kufasi, in which water seems not to fall so much as materialize out of thin air, only to be driven sideways by the wind. Caught in the open, the experience is as close to swimming on dry land as one is likely to get; it saturates clothes and skin and seems like it will drown you if you try to speak... or breathe.

The trick, then, is to not get caught in the open.

The storm blew up quickly — a little *too* quickly. The Land Rover with its passengers and supplies was halfway between Mji'na Bahari and M'Batha Station, bouncing along the rutted, single lane pathway they called a road, when the sky opened with a crack of thunder that shook the car windows and began dumping water on them. Instinctively, Mark Randall downshifted and slowed to a crawl, and now the vehicle was creeping along, almost as though they were feeling their way through the deluge. As they crept, tree branches bent under the weight of water and began slapping at the windshield with leafy hands.

The silence in the vehicle was almost as thick as the humid air, punctuated by the liquid slapping of the branches and the pounding of the sideways rain. There was a tacit silence from the passengers, unwilling to distract Mark from his task of driving, or perhaps contemplating the reality of their own mortality as the wheels spun in the mud and the Toyota slid through the ruts.

And then there was a muffled gasp from the front passenger seat.

Involuntarily, Mark took his eyes off the "road" long enough to glance at the source, then looked forward again. "Are you okay, Cassie?"

Cassidy Hudson had been peering out the windshield; she looked down, now, and said, "Yes, thanks. I'm sorry. I just had a — an epiphany, I guess. This reminded me of something — almost like *déjà vu*."

Mark smiled. "An epiphany?"

"It's nothing. It's hard to explain."

Mark was silent for half a mile or so, then said, "So which is it — nothing, or hard to explain?"

When she didn't respond immediately, one of the passengers in the back seat spoke up. "I'd like to hear it, Cassie."

"It's not that big a deal," she began, then sighed and shook her head. "Look, I'll tell you, but I don't want you to give me a hard time, okay?"

"Of course," Mark agreed seriously. "I would never give you a hard time."

"You would totally do it — but you promised, right?" When he agreed, she took a deep breath. "About a year and a half ago, I was sitting in church. The pastor was talking… and talking… and talking… and I guess I started to doze off, because all the sudden I felt like I was sitting in a car — and there were two other guys with me. I didn't know who they were, but they were both wearing white robes, and had long hair and beards. And we just sat there, while the car went through what seemed like an endless carwash — you know, the rollers, the brushes, the blowers. It just went on and on and then one of the men said to me, 'You know what you have to do.'"

She fell silent, then. Finally, Mark said, "I'll bite. What did you have to do?"

"I didn't know! And I said that — I said, 'What do you mean?' Then the *other* one spoke up and said, 'You must go to Africa. They are waiting for you.' And I said, 'Are you nuts? I can't go to Africa.' Then the first guy spoke up again, and he said, 'You know what you have to do.' And then I woke up." She paused again, lowered her voice until the people in the back seat could barely hear her. "Mama looked at me and asked what was wrong — said I looked like I'd seen a ghost. So I told her. You know what she said?"

"Don't sleep during church?" Mark guessed.

Cassie smiled. "She said, 'I guess you know what you have to do, Cassie girl.'" She shrugged. "So I did. I think it really was a calling, but it never made sense to me — why would I dream we were in a car wash? And then — just now — it hit me. The rollers and the brushed, the water — it was no car wash." She nodded toward the windshield, where the crawling of the car was dragging branches across the glass, like a car wash. "It was *this*. He, they — whoever — they were giving me a glimpse of the future, what it would be like. Do you think that's possible?"

"Well — weirder things have happened, haven't they?" Mark answered, without answering… and wondered. After a time, he said, "You know, we've all had our moment, when we realized that we were being called to this place. But yours is something special — you should feel blessed."

"I do," she said simply, and sat back with a smile on her face while the rain pounded on the windshield, and the branches brushed against the glass.

She was where she was supposed to be. Eventually, she would learn why.

Ash Wednesday

Matthew 6:1-6, 16-21

The Gift

Mason Randall stood silently, watching as the young woman set a piece of wood vertically on a stump, paused to take its measure, then raised and swung her axe down in one smooth, powerful motion that split the wood from top to bottom, causing each piece to fly off in opposite directions. She picked up another piece, went through the same motions, and split it with a solid *thunk* of sharpened steel meeting wood. He watched this another half-dozen times, then shook his head and said, "You're not being very reasonable about this, Miss Lee."

Without a word she dispatched another piece of wood, then paused for a breath and said, "I wasn't aware that I *had* to be reasonable, Mister Randall. Particularly in the face of such an *un*reasonable proposal." She mopped her brow as delicately as she could, tucked the kerchief into her sleeve, and began splitting firewood again.

He watched, again, until she stopped for a breath. "My client is offering to make a very generous donation, Miss Lee. I've been in your classroom, and I've seen the dormitory. I know that a gift of one thousand dollars would alleviate a lot of problems for you and for these children. You can't deny that." He paused, added shrewdly, "I certainly hope that you're not hesitating because these are *Indian* children."

Madeline Lee's eyes flashed and she swung the axe once more, buried the blade in the stump. She stood up straight, her eyes boring into his, and said, "Do you have children, Mister Randall?"

Puzzled, he shook his head in the slightest motion, back and forth.

"Then I suggest, for the sake of your hypothetical future children, you refrain from ever saying such a thing to me again. Ever." Her voice was quiet, but sharp as the axe she'd been swinging for the last half hour. He started to speak, but she held up a finger to stop him. "You are a very poor lawyer, Mister Randall. If you were a good one, you would have known that I spent the first few years of my life on this very reservation, when my father led the mission here, and my mother literally helped lay the foundation for the school. The parents of these children were my first friends."

"And your father and mother would be Reverend Jamison Lee, and Elizabeth, would they not?" he responded, equally quietly. "Don't presume to tell me how to do my job, Miss Lee. And if I offended you, I'm sorry — I didn't mean to imply anything except, perhaps, that you felt your children might not *need* the niceties that white children enjoy, back home."

"Niceties like books? Pencil and paper? Beds? As you say, you've been in my classroom, you know what it's like. We get by on precious little, Mister Randall, and it breaks my heart. It's broken my heart for the last three years."

"Then just imagine what you could do for them with a thousand dollars. A thousand dollars, US, for you to use however you wish. He could be here in just a couple of days, to personally give you that thousand dollars. Just imagine."

She sighed. "I *can* imagine, Mister Randall. Just as I can imagine that a rich, important man like your client, suddenly facing a lot of criticism for his predatory practices during this panic, not to mention virtually ruining the town of Grandeur, he might decide it was worth a thousand dollars to blunt that criticism. He might decide that making a gift to a school, properly publicized, would be just the thing for his image. Mightn't he, Mister Randall?"

Mason Randall folded his arms. "It's not my place to speculate on my client's motives, Miss Lee."

"Well, it *is* mine, Mister Randall. We're desperate, here — I won't try to convince you otherwise. But I'm not desperate enough to let *my* children be used as props for some kind of feel-good, public advertising spectacle. '*Prosechō mē poieō ho hymeis dikaiosynē emprosthen ho anthrōpos pros ho theaomai autos.*' 'Take care not to perform your good deeds before others so as to be seen by them.' Matthew 6:1."

The lawyer blinked. "Did you just speak *Greek* to me?"

In spite of herself, Madeline Lee smiled at his surprise. "I wasn't cursing."

"Oh, I know. I just —" He shook his head. "Never mind." He unfolded his arms. "Is that your final answer, then?"

"I cannot disrespect my children that way, Mister Randall. I will not let them — or myself — be used as stage props for your client."

He nodded slowly. "I understand. It's unfortunate, but I understand." He sighed, turned away and started to leave the schoolyard — then stopped at the gate, and turned back to her. "Miss Lee? Just hypothetically — if my client was to offer you the thousand dollars *without* making it a public gift... would you be willing to reconsider?"

It was her turn to blink, now. "I — you surprise me, Mister Randall. I don't for a moment believe you could get him to agree to it, but yes — if he would make this donation without making a public spectacle of it, we would welcome his generosity."

"Okay." He nodded, mostly to himself. "Okay." He smiled at the teacher, then. "Let me see if I can surprise you, Miss Lee. You'll be seeing me again."

Madeline Lee watched as the lawyer walked back to his buggy, and tried to decide if he was serious. It would have surprised her, a little, to know that he was trying to decide the same thing, himself.

Fortunately, he would have the long train ride back to Chicago to figure it out.

First Sunday in Lent

Mark 1:9-15

The Giver

"So this woman — this teacher — at the Lac des Morts Indian School... is she *slow*?" The speaker asked the question without turning his gaze from the panorama before them as they strolled along the midway. The Columbian Exposition — the so-called White City — lay like a jewel casually cast down along the shores of Lake Michigan, lit by what appeared to be a million light bulbs. And if that vista wasn't enough, the vision of the massive ferris wheel — more than twenty stories tall, capable of carrying thousands of passengers at a time — would surely take anyone's breath away.

Dominic Gauthier studied the view and saw money. Money spent building it, money taken in as people by the millions came from far and wide to see this miracle, and — most exciting of all — the prospect of future fortunes that would be won and lost by betting on the innovations that were part and parcel of the fair. Take electricity, for instance. It was all but a certainty, now, that it was going to be a permanent fixture in the urban landscape, but figuring out which way it was going to happen — would light be carried on the back of Edison's Direct Current, or Tesla's Alternating Current? — *that* was going to be a potential goldmine... or a disaster. The fair's developers had bet on Tesla, and his hastily developed light bulb, and that had turned out to be a winning wager — but what would the future bring?

He was pondering this when he realized his lawyer was talking. "What was that?" he asked, turning his eyes toward the young man, now.

Mason Randall refrained from rolling his eyes — he was *used* to repeating himself — and said simply, "No, sir, she's not slow. If anything, I would say she's extremely bright. And very opinionated, as well."

"And you explained to her that all I need — all I want her to do — is stand there and smile while I present her school with a thousand dollar

56

First Sunday in Lent

gift?"

"I did, sir. She views it as an attempt to grab favorable public mention, on your part, in response to your, uhm, troubles, sir."

Dominic Gauthier grunted and shook his head ruefully. "Had I known that shutting down that mill to break the union was going to lead to this much trouble, I would have thought about it a little longer. Of *course* it's a bid for good publicity. Any idiot — even a woman with her head in the clouds — could see that. The question is, what does it matter? It's the way the world works. Did you explain that to her?"

"I tried, sir. She would have none of it. She quoted scripture to me, sir — something about not performing your good deeds in front of others, so they can see." He smiled, just a flash of an expression. "In Greek, sir."

"Greek, eh? I don't care if she said it in the language of the Hottentots. She has no right to stand in my way." He fell silent, brooding as he watched the ferris wheel turn. Finally, he looked at his lawyer again. "Mason, you're young, and you're smart. You can go a very long way in this world if you don't let yourself get bogged down in moral questions. I want you to go back up there and break her. I don't care how you do it — bribery, blackmail, brute force — whatever it takes. Break her and bring her to heel, so she will accept my generous donation of five hundred dollars and do it with a smile for the reporters I'm going to bring with me."

"Five hundred dollars, sir?"

"Yes, five hundred. If she thought a thousand dollars gift was a little too gaudy, maybe five hundred will appeal to her conscience. And make sure she knows *why* it was reduced. We can't have people like her thinking they can stand against people of consequence. She has no particular corner on morality, here." For the first time, the client smiled, nodded to himself. "Yes, tell her that, exactly."

"With all due respect, sir, I don't think I can do that."

"Eh? Why not? You're a bright and persuasive man, a junior partner at one of the biggest law firms in the city of Chicago. If you will do what I say, I can virtually guarantee you that you will be a managing partner at that firm within just five years. They can use some strong new blood."

Mason Randall looked past his client to the White City, shook his head. "No, sir. I can't do that."

"Blast it, Randall, I have you and your firm on a fairly hefty retainer — I *own* your services."

The lawyer shrugged. "Maybe you do, sir. But you don't own my soul. That I get to keep for my very own. You need to stop asking me to do that, because I'm not going to. It's just that simple, sir."

"I will ruin you, Randall," Gauthier said bleakly.

"Well, sir, do what you think you must. But I'd rather have you ruin my reputation than tarnish my soul."

"Get out," Gauthier growled. "Go back to your firm and have them send me a real man."

Randall stood up, then, and bowed slightly. "I will pass along your message, Mister Gauthier. But it may not go the way you think it will. I think the managing partners down at the office believe the same thing I do — that a *real* man has a conscience."

"You keep thinking that. I've known most of them longer than you've been alive."

"But don't forget, sir — they've known *you*, too."

And with a tip of his hat, Mason Randall left.

Second Sunday in Lent

Mark 8:31-38

The Gift (Part 2)

Madeline Lee was writing on the blackboard with a stub of chalk when she heard the door of her classroom open. Without looking, she said, "Put them on the table, please," finished the sentence she was writing, and tapped the board with the chalk to make a period. Then, working off a piece of paper in her hand, she began writing in Menominee below the sentence. She was partway through the Menominee translation when she realized there had been no response to her greeting, and she turned toward the door.

What she saw made her hesitate. After a long silence, she cocked her head slightly and said, "Well, Mister Randall — whatever are you doing here? I would have thought you would be enjoying the fleshpots of civilization. I hear the world's Columbian Exposition is all the rage."

"It *is* something to see, Miss Lee — a spectacle for the eyes, and a feast for the senses." He looked around the school room. "Not that you will ever know. But I have been there and back. I didn't like the way our last conversation ended."

"You mean with a frank and honest discussion of your client's morals?"

He raised an eyebrow. "You didn't seem overly concerned about his morals when you agreed that you would take his thousand dollars donation, if he would donate it in private."

Her eyes flashed for the briefest moment, then she smiled. "*Touche*, Mister Randall. But, to be fair, I had no misapprehension that he would actually do so. No reflection on your lawyerly wiles, but I just know people like him."

He took a couple of steps toward her, then, paused with his hand resting on the back of a desk chair. "So do I. It's a funny thing, Miss Lee, but my father once told me that the downside of representing people with legal problems, is that they're people with legal problems. Not the cream of society, generally, nor of the most outstanding moral character. They are in the situations in which they find themselves, because they are flawed. We rarely find saints as clients."

Madeline started to answer, then stopped, put the chalk down and dusted the chalk dust off her hands. When she spoke, she was smiling. "It's a funny thing, Mister Randall — my father has said almost the same thing about the people *he* sometimes encounters in his ministry. I will concede your point. Nobody is perfect."

You're as close as I've ever seen to it, though — the thought flashed through Mason Randall's mind, and for an awkward moment he thought he'd said it out loud. When he realized he hadn't, he just nodded in agreement, stifled a sigh. "As you say, Miss Lee. I came back because I had promised to speak to my client, and I did — and he refused to consider making it a private donation. More words were had, but that was the gist of the conversation."

Madeline shrugged. "I am not surprised. But I thank you for trying to convince your client."

"Yes, of course — you're welcome. You made a very excellent point when we last met, that charity is best done without fanfare, lest it become something less seemly."

They stood for a moment or two, then, sizing one another up, neither sure where the conversation was going to go. Then, with another slight sigh, Mason reached into the small satchel he was carrying and pulled out a brown leather pouch. He walked to the front of the classroom, set the pouch on the teacher's desk, and stepped back, nodded toward it. "There," he said simply.

Madeline's eyebrows drew together, and she cocked her head again, reached for the pouch. "What?" she asked. Then she picked it up, opened it and looked inside — looked at her visitor again. "What is this?"

"Fifty double eagles, Miss Lee. I thought it best, rather than currency, what with all the uncertainty right now with banks."

She reached in, took out one of the gold coins and turned it over and over in her hand, studying it. "I thought your client said no?"

"He did — but I had another client who said yes."

"Who?"

Second Sunday in Lent

"An anonymous donor, Miss Lee. Surely you can appreciate the idea of anonymity in such affairs, all things considered."

"Oh, I can, I can — it's just that this is such a *generous* gift! I would like to be able to thank whoever it is."

"You may consider the donor thanked, Miss Lee. I hope this will help you and the children."

She put the coin back into the pouch, cinched it shut. "It will, trust me. It will."

"Good." He paused, shifted the satchel to his other hand. "Now that my legal duties have been discharged, I wonder if you could tell me, Miss Lee — is there something around here that I can do for you — for the school, I mean?"

Madeline set the coins aside. "What do you mean, Mister Randall?"

He sighed deeply, this time. "I mean, I've seen what you are doing here, and what you are up against. You are surely doing God's work, and I would like to help you with it, if you will have me?"

"You mean you want to *move* here?" Her voice was incredulous.

He just nodded.

"What about Chicago? The Exposition? City life?"

He shrugged. "It occurred to me, Miss Lee, that I don't think I can be comfortable anymore, knowing how people here are struggling. Not unless I'm doing something to at least try to help. '*Gar tis opheleo anthropos kerdaino ho holos kosmos, kai ho autos psyche?*'"

The teacher nodded, then translated. "'What does it profit a man to gain the whole world, yet forfeit his life?' I understand. But do you — really?"

Mason Randall smiled. "For the first time in my life, I think I do."

Third Sunday in Lent

John 2:13-22

A Turn Of The Tables

There was a wind sighing through the Kidron Valley as they walked. For what seemed like a very long time, it was the only sound other than their footsteps and the faint echo of the throngs of pilgrims across the valley in Jerusalem. Finally, Peter cleared his throat. "Do you want to talk about it?" he tested.

Without changing his gait, or turning to look at Peter, Jesus answered, "No."

A brief pause, this time. Then, "You have to talk about it some time, teacher."

Jesus glanced at him, this time, a quick look out of the corner of his eye. "Actually, no, I don't have to."

"But —"

"There is nothing you can say that can *possibly* compel me to 'talk about it.'" Jesus said, turning his eyes forward again. One of the other disciples started to say something, but Peter flashed a look at him, shook his head, and the comment was swallowed. Finally, as they drew near to Mary and Martha's house, Jesus said softly, "I just *snapped*. It was like something inside of me just caught fire, all of a sudden, and I couldn't stop it."

Peter nodded. "Yeah, I got that. It was something to see — once."

Jesus sighed; visions of flipping tables and scattering coins, doves and pigeons suddenly set free, doves fluttering around the courtyard in confusion while sheep bleated and ran for their lives, flashed through his mind. He shook his head, as though to banish them, and said, "It's just that, all of a sudden — I don't know why — but it was like I was seeing the merchants and the moneychangers for the first time, and they *incensed* me. I thought, 'Why should someone coming to temple have to *buy* something in order to worship here?' And allowing people in my father's house to make money when they changed coins so pilgrims could donate to the temple… it just seemed so *wrong*. I couldn't stand it."

"I think I can safely say you got your point across," Peter said dryly.

Behind them, along the road, someone snickered — both men whipped their heads around to glare, and it stopped at once.

"The thing is, I'm not wrong," Jesus continued, after a couple of steps. "What I saw up there — what's been going on there for *years* — is wrong. It focuses on the letter of the law, and not the spirit — a man who needs to make a sacrifice, now doesn't have to offer up his own, he just has to buy one. Instead of offering to return to our Father something that has been raised and nurtured with care, that a person has a connection to, it's just one more thing that can be bought. I tell you, Father doesn't *need* the sacrifice — he's concerned with the spirit behind it, the thought and meaning. It's like buying a trinket for your mother, instead of making her something with your own hands."

Peter let that idea roll around in his head for a bit, then nodded. "I can see why it would make you angry, then."

"And don't even get me started on the moneychangers. By selling concession space to them, the temple priests are just participating in the crime."

"And yet, Master, these people are just earning their livelihood. I know you have nothing against that. In fact, you feel quite strongly that workers should be paid for their efforts. If I remember correctly, you told me I was going to hell that time I didn't tip that waitress in Capernaum."

Jesus' eyebrows arched. "Really? Aren't we exaggerating just a little?"

"Well — maybe a little. But you did practically accuse me of taking food out of her children's mouths."

"And I was right. People have a right to earn a living. They have a right to earn money. But what they don't have is a right to earn money by engaging in questionable practices. And, my friend, using God's name to help you make sales is a questionable practice. Nor do they have a right to capitalize on someone's religious beliefs for the purpose of making money. This is no gray area — it is a matter of fact."

"Hence your tantrum, back at the temple."

Jesus shrugged. "I hardly think it was a tantrum, Peter. It was righteous indignation. People need to understand what's going on — Father is loving and grace filled, but he is not to be trifled with. If you are going to do evil, do it in *your* name, not his. At least have the courage to be honest about what you're doing."

"And the hyperbole about rebuilding the temple, Master? I've seen miraculous signs, but even you — rebuilding what has taken half a century to build, in just three days..." Peter shook his head. "I don't know — that's a lot to accept, isn't it?"

They were at the gateway to the house, now, and Jesus stopped short. While the disciples drew close, he waited patiently — then he smiled a mysterious, almost wistful smile and reached out, put a hand on Peter's shoulder. "Just remember — not all temples are made of stone, my friend."

And before Peter or any of the others could ask for an explanation, Jesus passed through the gate.

Fourth Sunday in Lent

John 3:14-22

Here Comes The Judge

Dinner was over. It had been a strained meal — in days past, when Jesus had partaken in a formal meal in someone's home, the guests had mostly kept quiet, the better to listen to the discourse between Jesus and his innermost disciples, or the occasional visitor with the temerity to question him on some fine point of the law. Tonight, everyone seemed to be talking about what had happened that afternoon in the temple courtyard. Those who had been there and those who had not seemed equally sure of the details, and none of them seemed to want to press Jesus about it, although they were happy to discuss it among themselves.

Jesus took it in in silence.

Martha began to clear the table, and some of the other women joined her. Jesus looked to his right, nudged Mary with his foot and caught her eye, nodded toward her sister. She bowed her head, stood up and started to pick up dishes, speaking softly to the other women as they worked. When that conversation moved toward the kitchen, Jesus sighed and picked up a piece of bread that had fallen on the table.

"Everyone seems to know what happened except me," he said quietly to Peter, sitting to his left. He turned his head toward Peter, started to speak, then twisted his whole body around until he could look at him more easily. "Everybody seems to know why I went off the way I did. It was stress. It was fatigue. It was an argument with the priests. It was an argument with the Pharisees. It was an argument with *you*. Everybody seems to know — but no one really does."

"Maybe you should explain it to them — tell them what you told me, earlier," Peter offered.

Jesus shrugged. "It hardly matters. People will form their own opinions, no matter what I say. You can share what I said with your brothers and the others as you wish, but my purpose here is not to explain everything I do or say in detail."

"If it's any comfort, you're still doing that pretty well."

Jesus said nothing.

"You look like you're still mad," Peter said.

Jesus sighed deeply, lifted his hand and covered his eyes. "That would probably be because I still am."

"At us? At them?" Peter asked hopefully.

Jesus rubbed his eyes and lowered his hand, sighed again. "I'm angry, because I'm angry."

Peter frowned, scratched his head. "Didn't your Mom and Dad ever teach you that 'just because' is not a valid reason?"

"They did. But that's not what I'm talking about. I'm saying that I'm angry because I *got* angry. That I've been angry."

"You had reason, Master — you explained it yourself, you had good reason."

"But that's just it, Peter — it doesn't matter how good a reason I had." He fell silent, closed his eyes, then opened them again and took a deep breath. "Who am I, Peter?"

Peter looked at his friend and teacher, frowned. "You're the Messiah, Master."

He smiled, then. "Yes, my friend — I *am* the Messiah. And I am your redeemer — humanity's redeemer — sent by my Father. And that means I was not sent to judge or to condemn the world, but to *save* humanity from judgment — to show you God's kingdom, to show you love. What I did this afternoon was... not what I came to do."

"So you're angry at yourself?"

"Yes."

There was a long silence, then Peter said, "You're aware of the irony, I assume?" When Jesus looked at him sharply, he added, "You know — that you are judging yourself for judging others?"

Jesus shook his head. "This is not a time for your sense of humor, Peter. I have a mission, a reason for being here, and I'm not sure I can do it the way I'm supposed to. My temper —"

"Your righteous indignation."

"Whatever. It concerns me."

"It doesn't concern me." When Jesus said nothing, Peter leaned toward him and lowered his voice. "Look, I'm serious. You have taught us so much — the words of the prophets come alive when you speak them, and God's love for us... we can *feel* it when you speak. And we can see it when you act. And we also know that you have no patience for injustice, or for people who twist the word of God. The fact that that showed through this one day... this one time... it doesn't speak to your judgment of those people, but to your love for God. The very love that you have tried so hard to share with us." He leaned even closer, then, lowered his voice almost to a whisper. "I know you have a lot on your mind right now, I can sense it. You know that something big is going to happen, and this — it just took you by surprise."

Jesus frowned. "Do you really think so?"

Peter nodded. "I know so. You are here to bring light to the world — not to judge it. Any fool can see that, if I can."

Jesus smiled, then, and reached out, put his hand over Peter's. "Bless you, Peter. I chose my rock well. Thank you."

Peter placed his other hand on top of their hands and smiled in return. "And we chose our teacher well. Now... teach us something about your Father's kingdom."

Fifth Sunday in Lent

John 12:20-33

The Appointed Hour

Philip threaded his way through the crowd, moving from the outer edge to a place closer to the center, where Andrew was engaged in a discussion of some kind with two men. As he neared, the strangers laughed at something that Andrew had said. Philip hesitated, then touched Andrew on the arm. Andrew excused himself, turned away from the two strangers and looked at Philip curiously. "Yes, Brother?"

Philip looked around for a moment to get his bearings, then pointed toward a trio of men standing together at the edge of the crowd. "We have visitors," Philip said. "Greeks, from the Decapolis. Hippus, I think." He looked directly at Andrew, then. "They want to meet the Master."

Andrew stared across the crowd, at the trio, no expression on his face. Then he turned his eyes back to Philip. "Why?"

"They've heard of him, back in the Decapolis. And they heard him earlier today, speaking. So they want to see him. They have questions."

Andrew chuckled. "Tell them to get in line."

Philip shook his head. "No, brother. They've heard him talking about our Lord, and they — as near as I can tell — they are questioning their own beliefs in their own gods. They want to know more."

Andrew sighed. "Well, I'm sure he would be happy to explain. Maybe."

Philip frowned. "'Maybe?'"

"It's not been a good day, brother. He is talking about — you know," he said evasively, unwilling to say it.

"Death?" Philip guessed, filling in the blank.

Another sigh. "Death. Betrayal. Suffering. You know how it is when he starts down that path."

Now it was Philip's turn to sigh, and both men stood in silence. After years of ministry, it was difficult to see the Master become as dark as he had, lately. Where there had been signs and wonders, there were now

Fifth Sunday in Lent

more parables; where his words had been about love, and grace, and mercy, they were now about his own impending suffering and death — apparently the end point that had been planned all along for his ministry.

Among themselves, in the dark of the night, more than one of the disciples had openly wondered if the stress of constant conflict with the establishment had grown to be too much for him. The optimistic, world-beating early days were a memory, now, replaced by intense teachings and somber reflections on mortality.

And yet, nobody was talking about going home; none of the twelve, or the others who had attached themselves to his ministry, were ready to go back to life before Jesus. It was just that they were beginning to have a sense of how it was going to end — and it was not a pretty picture. Without a lot of hope, Andrew nodded his head toward the center of the crowd, where Jesus was holding forth to a small group of priests who had come to hear his message for themselves — or to report back to the high priest any heresies they heard.

It was hard to tell which.

"Let's go see if he has time to speak to them," Andrew said. "They're not of us — this might cheer him up, to know that Gentiles are starting to hear his message." Without waiting for an answer, he started toward Jesus, cutting a direct line through the crowded courtyard, with Philip in tow. It took a minute or two before they were standing by his side; as they approached, he dismissed the priests, turned his attention to them.

"Andrew... Philip," he said quietly, and once again Andrew was struck by the feeling that, in that moment of time, Jesus was directing his full focus on them. There were rarely any idle moments in his presence — if you were there, he was paying attention to you without question or hesitation, as though you actually mattered. It could be flattering, and unsettling, but eventually you got used to it.

Almost.

"What can I do for you?" he asked and waited.

Andrew and Philip glanced at one another, then Andrew answered. "Master, there are three men here from the Decapolis. They want to speak with you." He smiled. "They want to ask about what you've been teaching — and about our Lord, and the kingdom of heaven."

Jesus looked at the men, then back to his disciples. "They're Greeks?"

"I assume so. As you see, they are not dressed like us. And they told our brother, here, that they wanted to ask about their own gods, as well."

Jesus nodded. "I see." Jesus raised his eyes to the heavens, then, and held out his hands, palms up, in an attitude of prayer. "Heavenly Father, the appointed hour has arrived for me. The son of man has reached both Jew and non-Jew, to show them your kingdom, so the die has been cast. Lord, let me be lifted up before *all* people, so they might be saved."

Philip frowned. "Umm — I'm not sure what that means."

"I have come to bring life to *all* humanity, but just as a seed must die and be buried to bear fruit, so must I, too, fall and die, and be buried in the ground to fulfill the redemption of these, my people. When I am lifted up for all to see, I will lift up *all* people with me."

Philip and Andrew listened, tried to speak a couple of times, but Jesus just kept going. Philip listened to Jesus until he was done, then took a breath, started to speak — and Jesus turned away, began speaking to someone else. They waited a short time, then Andrew caught Philip's eye and pointed back the way they had come with his head.

As they made their way back toward the Greeks, Andrew said quietly, "We need to talk to our Master, Philip. We need to understand what is going on — why he's acting this way."

"D'you think?" Philip asked sarcastically, felt instantly sorry. Something profound was obviously happening to Jesus, and they just couldn't get a handle on it. "Maybe he's just trying to wrap his head around that welcome he got, today — the palm leaves, and the hosannas. It's quite a contrast to what he *thinks* is going to happen."

"Maybe," Andrew agreed, without really embracing the idea. Then he shook his head and added, "We're all doing dinner on Thursday — just us disciples and him. Maybe that would be a good time to ask — to tell him that we're worried."

"I think so," Philip agreed, then frowned. "But in the meantime — did Jesus say he would meet the Greeks, or not?"

Liturgy of the Passion

Mark 14:1-15:47

Judas (Part 1)

Albert sat in the land cruiser and looked at the M'Batha mission station. In the months since he had come with the Americans — well over a year, now — it had been brought back to life, even expanded. There were beds in the medical clinic, where patients could spend the night and be tended by nurses or one of *two* doctors, and there was talk of a portable x-ray machine being brought in. There were also two classrooms, where villagers could be taught by the nurses, and three examination rooms.

Across the compound from the clinic was the chapel and mission school, still a combination of permanent and temporary structures. There, weekly worship services were held along with still more classes for those who were interested in learning more about the European god. More than once, he had caught Mark Randall just standing in the middle of the compound, taking it all in, and smiling like a man who had been given a great gift.

"Admit it, my young friend," a voice said from the back seat, "You've seen it for yourself. They're killing our people."

He shook his head. "No."

"Yes," the voice said, and Albert closed his eyes, not wanting to see the leathery, scornful face of Djimon looking back at him in the rearview mirror. Unseen, the voice continued to whisper. "You see it everyday, don't you? Your white friends steal the essence of our people a little more every day. If you watch the faces of the desperate people who come to the medical building, you can see them losing their grip on the truth… embracing the scandalous lies of these outsiders."

He opened his eyes, then, and looked at the mirror — at the Mganga's face. "They came here to help, Djimon. They heal the sick and teach us about Jesus."

Djimon smiled scornfully. "They came here to show us western ways, and to drag us away from our ancestors. They don't care about us — they care about making themselves feel powerful. They care about making our people doubt the true ways. They care only about the darkness within their souls. Let them make us weak with their medicine… let them distract us with their impossible God… and the day will come when they will take the very land from us and make us their slaves. That is how they plan to 'help' us."

Albert shook his head again, though his heart was uncertain. "No, they're not like that. They care — they really do care."

"If they cared — if they knew as much as they claim they do — then why hasn't the doctor cast out the demon from Chuma? Instead, he makes him dependent on some white medicine that only they can provide."

"Chuma has something wrong with his brain that causes him to collapse, shake, and froth — not a demon."

"That's what they tell you — so instead of casting out the demon with a spell, they can keep him captive to their medicine." Djimon leaned forward, placed a hand on Albert's shoulder. "Everything they do strips away what we know and replaces it with something foreign and strange. This is no way for people to live, Albert — in fear, in thrall to these white interlopers."

Albert thought about all that he had seen — compared it to the uneasiness in his own heart as they seemed to slip further and further away from tradition and the old knowledge. They had gone down that road once, and the Europeans had dominated them for generations. What if this was just a more subtle approach to the same end?

And what if he was helping them do it?

"What would you have me do, Djimon?" he asked, barely whispering.

"I have a friend who knows someone with the People's Liberation Brigade. With one word from me, I can have the BLPK here by tonight, and they will burn the clinic to the ground. And the church." Djimon paused, let it sink in. "One word, Albert, and everything they've done to our people can be *un*done. And then they will leave, because they know we are too powerful to let them enslave us."

Albert shook his head. "The constabulary will never let the rebels do that."

"And that is where *you* come in, Albert. If you were to tell them that you are just back from a visit to Mlima Mbali — and that you encountered a squad of BLPK soldiers on your way here — there would be no constabulary to worry about. They would be off to Mlima Mbali, hunting rebels. And *that* would allow our true friends to come here and burn down the clinic, chase away the missionaries. All it takes is a word from someone they trust… and they trust you, don't they, my young friend?"

Albert closed his eyes, rested his head on the headrest and let the thoughts swirl inside him for a while. It was true enough, he thought, that he could see a change in the people of M'Batha — no longer sure of the old ways, of what they *thought* they knew, they were beginning to adopt the ways of the missionaries. If it went too far, they would lose themselves — who they were.

And that was a steep price to pay for some antibiotics and a sermon on Sunday.

"Are you sure you can do this?" he asked, opening his eyes — but there was no one in the back seat.

That made the decision for him. He started the land cruiser, slipped it into gear, and drove down the road to the Constabulary Station on the outskirts of the village. As he drove, he rehearsed his story of an encounter with BLPK bandits on the road from Mlima Mbali.

It was the right thing to do.

Maundy Thursday

John 13:1-17, 31-35

Judas (Part 2)

Confusion.
Fear.
Overpowering uncertainty.

They swelled and collided, they danced in his gut while Albert stood in the center of the clinic waiting room, immobile. Outside, there were shouts and screams as AK-47s belched bullets into the air in long, pointless bursts; the smell of smoke was already heavy as the church burned on the far side of the compound, engulfed in an inferno that could never be extinguished.

Cassidy Hudson came through the front door, slammed it, and locked it. "They're shooting people out there! Men in camouflage — I don't know who they are!"

"People's Liberation Brigade — they're supposed to be under control in this province," Mark Randall said. His voice seemed remarkably calm — a contrast to his frenetic actions as he pulled patient files out of the cabinets and dumped them into a wastebasket. "I guess they're not," he added, and paused long enough to smile briefly at Cassidy and the other staff who had started to gather.

"I guess not," Tom Brown agreed. "What are you doing with my charts?"

"Destroying them."

"No!" It was an automatic response.

"Yes. If these rebels act the way they have in the past, they're liable to go after anyone who's come here for treatment. If we can destroy the records, we can keep the villagers safe." He stopped for a moment, looked around the room at the faces, staring at him, then singled out one of them and said to her, "Take this to the bathtub, dump them in."

She hesitated just for a moment, then grabbed the wastebasket and took it to one of the treatment rooms — and the only bathtub for a hundred miles — while Mark finished emptying the cabinet.

When the last of the files went in, Tom Brown grabbed the basket and said, "I've got this," hurried toward the exam room.

"Use alcohol to get it going," Mark added.

"What else should we do?" Cassidy asked, eyes wide.

"We stay in here. Well — *we* do." He looked around the room — all of the foreigners seemed to be there, along with Albert, a handful of patients, and several locals who had begun working at the mission. "The rest of you — people from here — you need to leave. Out the back door, if it's not covered by the rebels. Albert, tell them."

"No!" Albert shot back. "*Everyone* needs to leave. If we all leave, we will all be safe. I'm sure of it."

"Tell your people, Albert." Mark glanced around the room again, catching the eyes of his companions, and saw no argument. "We're going to stay — you're going to leave. From what I understand, anyone who is connected to us will be in danger, and that's not what we came here to do. We're here to serve you, not put you in danger. But you have to go now, while you have a chance."

Albert seemed about to argue, then started gesturing to the locals and speaking rapidly. It didn't seem to take much convincing — they moved toward the back of the clinic, and what they hoped was a safe exit facing the jungle. Albert dd not immediately follow them, but moved when Mark did. "I can't leave you here," Albert repeated. "We must all leave, in order to be safe."

"There is no safe for us, my friend — but we can help you one last time." They were at the back exit, then, lined up in a short hallway. Mark squeezed past the natives, went to the door and looked out the small rectangular window in the metal sheathed door. After what seemed like minutes, at least, he stood back and said, "It looks clear, for the moment. The nine of you make a break for it — run once you're outside, until you're in the tree line. Then go back to your homes and lay low. Albert, you're going to have to try to stay out of their way."

Albert relayed what he said, then squeezed past and opened the door. They pushed their way out the door and ran for cover — thankfully, there was no gunfire. When the others were gone, Mark ushered Albert out the door with a sweep of his hand. When he just stood there, Mark frowned. "You have to do this, Albert. We'll be okay. The rebels may even be content with just burning the church."

As though in answer to the statement, there was another burst of gunfire from out front, and more screams.

"I don't think they will be," Albert said with quiet urgency. "It is not safe for you here."

Mark put a hand on his shoulder. "We didn't come here to be safe, my friend — we came here to serve. To serve *you*. So that's what's going to happen, and we'll get together when this is all over, okay?"

Hating himself for it, Albert let himself be sent away. But in the doorway, he paused long enough to turn to Mark and stammer, "I'm sorry."

Mark's smile was ghostly. "I know."

He closed the door and locked it to force his friend to safety.

Good Friday

John 18:1-19:42

A Final Rest

You can make an argument to the contrary — and many have — but the sheer urge to kill and destroy is not primal in most people. Made in God's image, most people retain at least enough of that image to not *want* to wantonly destroy whatever is set before them without provocation. That being said, the irony is that once the switch is flipped, it can be hard to turn: off something like a simple raid to intimidate foreigners and remind the locals that there is still an active resistance movement can quickly turn into something much more.

The orgy of destruction and bloodshed did not end until morning came to M'Batha. A pall of smoke hung over the village, and the air was thick with the smell of charred wood and shattered dreams. M'Batha Station was nothing but ruins now, here and there a structural member still stood upright, supporting nothing, but for the most part the fires had leveled the compound. Along with the omnipresent ash, there was debris everywhere — papers, books, ripped up mattresses, some pieces of medical equipment deemed too uninteresting to loot…

And, front and center of the clinic, there was a lump lying on the ground, man-sized but otherwise hard to distinguish from everything else that lay there as mute testimony to madness.

Outside what had been the walls of the compound, a handful of villagers stood and surveyed what remained of the foreigners' mission, whispered among themselves and occasionally poked one another with an elbow, to point toward something that caught their eye. More than one pointed to the lump on the ground and shook their head, tut-tutting in hushed tones as though afraid anything louder might summon the evil back.

Finally, a figure broke from the villagers and stepped onto the mission grounds.

Immediately, a taller, thin figure stepped forward and grabbed him by the shoulder. "Chuma!" she exclaimed, "What are you doing?"

The boy looked up at his mother and said, "I'm going to help Mister Mark."

She looked away for a moment, then back at her son. "There is no help for him," she said firmly. "He is dead. Life has left his body."

"I know," Chuma answered, with the grave expression of a ten-year old who had already seen more death than he should have. "But he was our friend. He and Doctor Tom came here to help. We can't just leave him like that. Doctor Tom would not have wanted it."

"Doctor Tom is not here," his mother answered reasonably. He and the other foreigners had been bound and dragged to a truck and driven away — she did not dare to think about what might be happening to them even now.

"All the more reason that *we* should help him," her son answered, just as reasonably. He looked her in the eye, then. "Mother, when I was sick, would you have wanted me to be left alone in the dirt, like that? Or would you have wanted someone to help me?"

"But he's not sick, he's *dead*!" she answered with inexorable logic — then realized that her voice had gone up and was immediately embarrassed. This was not a time or place for loud voices, standing among the ruins, in the presence of death.

Chuma's response was silent and could have come from any child on any continent, in any age: he shrugged, and twisted slightly so her hand dropped away from his shoulder. Then, free, he set out toward the body in the middle of the compound. His mother watched, but did not move to help or hold him back.

Of their own accord, his steps started to slow as he drew near to the body — then, conscious of being watched, Chuma straightened his back a little and quickened his pace. Once there, he hesitated, looked down, and said softly, "God I do not know, watch over this man. He was your good servant, and a friend to us." He paused, still looking down, and added, "And give me strength," for he suddenly realized how *big* Mark Randall had been.

Then, with a sigh, he squatted down on a bit of dry earth, where blood had not seeped, and reached out, struggled to roll the body over.

Chuma's eyes closed as he pushed, then he forced them open and looked at what remained of Mister Mark.

There was dried blood on his face, the beginning of swelling around one eye, and a wound on the side of his head into which Chuma chose not to look, but the hair on that side of his head was matted and sticky. It appeared that one of his shoulders was out of joint — Chuma knew what that looked like, because it had happened to one of his cousins — and the front of his shirt was covered in blood and dirt. When Chuma summoned the courage to stop taking inventory and actually look at the man's face, he saw that Mister Mark's eyes were open — but the eyes and the face did not convey fear, which fit Chuma's recollection of the event, as much as he could see from where he had been hiding.

"You were a good man," he whispered, and reached out, gently closed his eyes.

With a sigh, he stood up, brushed the dirt from his legs, and considered the body before him. He already knew where he wanted to bury him but getting him there had not been part of the hastily conceived plan. Uncertainly, he reached down and grabbed the collar of his shirt, began to pull....

The body barely moved.

When he had dragged the body just a few feet, he stopped, straightened up, and looked down at it, hands on hips. He was still staring when he noticed a shadow on the ground next to his. Startled, he looked up, saw a girl — tall, lanky, from a village nearby; he didn't know her name. "Kesi," she said, answering his unspoken question. "Mister Mark brought food to my family when my father was ill and sat with us when he died."

No sooner had she said that, than a boy about his age stepped up next to her. He said nothing, just looked at Chuma and rolled up his own sleeve, exposing the ring of a smallpox vaccination. Together, then, with Kesi lifting his shoulders and Chuma and the other boy each lifting by one leg, they were able to pick Mark up and carry him to the place Chuma had picked out.

A place their friend could rest.

Resurrection of the Lord

John 20:1-18

Ghosts

"Dad?"

"One second, the water's running," John Randall answered, and methodically finished rinsing the bowl in his hands before setting it in the drying rack and turning off the water. He picked up the towel hanging over the edge of the sink, turned and wiped his hands, then leaned back against the counter. "Whatcha need, Bud?"

"Do we believe in ghosts?"

You just never know what he's going to ask, John thought, and raised an eyebrow. "'We' who? We, as a family — or the church?"

Mark hesitated — it wasn't a difference he thought about very often, being a pastor's child. "Family, I guess. I mean, what do *you* think?" Then, after a beat, he added, "Cause that's what the church thinks, too, right?"

"Well, that's an interesting question. Let me flip the order. The church doesn't think much about ghosts, in general. We mostly don't talk about them, but we do hold by scripture, which condemns witchcraft and summoning spirits and that kind of thing, so let's just say we're not fans. And one of Jesus' parables — you remember the rich man and Lazarus? — indicates that God doesn't allow the dead to come back and talk to the living, but that wasn't the point of the parable, so we don't know how much faith to put in that. But we're not totally comfortable with the subject, so we don't say much."

"Sort of like you and that birds and bees talk we had?"

John smiled slightly, shrugged in agreement. "Fair enough, I guess."

"So what do *you* think?"

"I think there are more things we don't understand than things we do. In all of human experience, ghosts and such are consistent across all societies, in all places, in one way or another. So I'm not going to rule them out. And I'm not going to rule them in. I just think we don't know.

Maybe we never will." He wiped his hands again, and set the towel on the counter. "Why do you ask? Are you watching reruns of *One Step Beyond* again?"

His son grinned sheepishly. "No, I've learned my lesson there. No, it's just —" He looked over his shoulder. "Where's Mom?"

"She's taking Grandma Newman and her sister back to their hotel. Why?"

Mark glanced down, licked his lips, looked up again. "I saw — I *think* I saw Grampa Newman. Today. At church."

"Oh." He didn't say anything more.

"It was after I got confirmed — when we were going through the handshaking thing."

"The reception line?"

"Yeah. We were going through the reception line, and I was just so — relieved. I was talking to Bonnie Burnett, and we got to the end of the line, and the last guy said, 'Congratulations, Mark, I'm proud of you.' And he seemed really familiar, but I wasn't paying attention — and then after I stepped away, I realized why. His voice — it was Grampa's voice. And he smelled like Old Spice, like Grampa wore. But when I turned around, he was already walking out the door, I just saw him from the back. But it looked like him... from the back, I mean."

"Did Bonnie see him?" John tried to be matter of fact, not judgmental.

Mark shook his head. "No, Dad — well, she didn't remember. But she didn't know him, and we shook a lot of hands this morning. Why is that?"

"Different question. Let's stay on this. You saw your grandfather, but only from the back, right?"

"Right, But I *heard* him, sure as shooting — and I *smelled* him. I'm sure of it."

John shrugged. "I'm not going to say you didn't. I didn't, and your Mom and sister didn't, but you were the one going down the reception line. I'm willing to say that that's what you think you saw, without a doubt."

"So I saw a ghost?"

"Like I said, that's certainly what you think you saw. I'm convinced."

"But not convinced that I really saw him?" Mark probed.

"I think the human mind is capable of creating extraordinary things in here," he answered, tapping his head with his finger. "In times of great stress, or happiness, we can see what we want to see, or even hope to see. And it's real, in most senses of the word. It's real for you."

"Dad, it's either real or it's not. 'Real for you' is just a way of saying I was seeing things."

John hesitated, tapping a finger on the counter behind him, then said, "Let me tell you something. My dad — your Grampa Randall — died in 1952, right after I got back from Vaca Muerto. Before I finished seminary. You never knew him, of course, but he had this cough — he'd had it all his life, because he smoked like a chimney, unfiltered Camels. It was a habit he picked up in the war, and he never kicked it. But the point is, it was very distinctive. You know how some people have that, right? They can cough, or clear their throat, and even if your eyes were closed, you'd know it was them?"

"Sure, Maggie sneezes like that. It's like —"

"Later. The point is, I knew that cough. And on the day I was ordained, standing up there, taking my vows, in front of a church full of maybe three hundred people — I heard that cough. I mean, that exact cough. May as well have said his name, instead."

Mark looked puzzled. "You *heard* Grampa Randall?"

John nodded. "I was so nervous that when I heard it, I couldn't turn around to look, but I know it was him, as surely as I know anything. But after a little bit, I wasn't nervous anymore, because I knew my Dad was there, watching — that he was proud of me, no matter what disagreements we'd had. I knew he loved me, and that he was there to see me start a new life in God. Now, I never saw him — I don't know if anybody did. And I don't know if anybody else heard him. But I know *I* did, and it made that day even more special. So you can't tell me I was just hearing things — and I certainly can't tell you. I can't tell you what I think about ghosts, but I can tell you that I totally believe that once in a while, for a specific reason, a loving God might allow this world and the next to touch, for a window to be opened, if only for a few moments… and that's something very special. Call it a ghost, call it a window —

call it a miracle. It's special."

"Do you think it would be okay to tell Mom?"

John smiled. "I think she would be very happy to hear it."

He nodded agreement, turned to leave and stopped, turned back to him. "So Grampa Newman is sort of like Jesus, right? He came back for a very special reason, too — you talked about it last Easter. He showed himself to people so they would know he wasn't dead, that even dying the way he did wasn't the end."

John nodded slowly. "I wouldn't want to take the similarities too far — but okay, sure. The same — but with differences."

"I can think of one right now," Mark said. When his father looked at him questioningly, he grinned and said, "I'll bet Jesus never said 'pull my finger.'"

"Probably not," John agreed with a warm smile. "Now go finish your homework."

Second Sunday of Easter

John 20

Ghosts (Part 2)

Tom Brown looked around the clearing, taking in the markers and stones, which seemed to be placed at random, and shook his head. He looked down at the patch of earth at his feet and frowned, finally looked at the teenager who had brought him there. "Chuma — are you sure this is it?" Apart from four fist-sized stones marking out a rectangle, there was nothing to set it apart from the rest of the grassy clearing.

He watched the youth's face as the man from the FSK — Kufasi Security Forces — translated. He caught a few words in the rapid-fire exchange, but it was the boy nodding his head that gave the answer before it was translated. The soldier looked at Tom and nodded. "He is sure, Doctor Brown."

"What makes him so sure?"

Tom looked down at the man standing next to him, leaning on a pair of canes. Once upon a time he had been taller than Tom; now he was hunched over, an arthritic old man of 29, beaten down by the years. He looked up at Tom, shrugged. "It's a valid question. To me, one patch of dirt looks pretty much like the other in this... place." He hesitated over the last word, glanced at the soldier.

Tom nodded, turned back to the soldier. "My brother has a point. How can he be sure it's the right spot?"

The soldier spoke to Chuma, and there was a brief exchange. The soldier then took a couple of steps back and looked at the ground, brushed aside some grass with his foot and toed a rock about the size of a soccer ball. He bent over to look at it more closely, nodded to himself. "The boy says it is next to his father's grave," he explained to Tom, "and here is the marker for his father."

"I see." Tom looked at Chuma. "I'm sorry, Chuma."

The teenager bobbed his head.

The soldier looked past Tom, then, raised his hand as a signal to

Second Sunday of Easter

two villagers standing at the edge of the clearing, leaning on shovels, waiting while the foreigners were taken to the grave they sought. As the two men approached, Chuma spoke to the soldier. There was a short conversation, then the soldier said, "The boy asks why are you disturbing your friend's grave?"

"I told you he didn't get it," Barry Brown muttered to his brother.

Tom ignored the comment. "Please tell him that we want to take Mark's remains back to his family. It's been five years since he — passed away. They could use the closure."

"This his home," Chuma answered directly. "We his family."

"His family would not have killed him, or stood by while he was killed," Barry responded bitterly.

Tom looked down at his brother and said quietly, "The villagers — Chuma and his friends — saw to it that he had a decent burial. They didn't kill him, but they couldn't have stopped it — you saw what it was like." To Chuma and the soldier he said, "I understand what you're saying, and we are grateful for your help — for everything you did. But his father and his mother... his sister — his friends — would like him to come home. His church would like to put him to rest properly."

Chuma spoke rapidly, then, and the guard translated as the men began to dig. "His home is here, Doctor Tom. His church is here. They were right over there." The teen pointed toward the ruins of the mission station, barely visible through the trees surrounding the clearing. "Your clinic was there. All there. This was home, for him. For you."

"We lost all that five years ago, didn't we?" Barry Brown challenged. "You have no right."

A thick silence fell over them, then, broken only by the sounds of the two villagers lifting a layer of rocks that were just under the dirt they had scraped off the ground. Once the rocks were moved, they began to dig in earnest, the shovels making regular, rhythmic chuffing sounds as they sliced into the sandy soil. Tom Brown stepped away, unwilling to watch too closely, unsure of when the men would begin to strike his friends remains. Chuma, too, stepped away, clearly agitated.

They stood side by side, both staring toward the old mission station. Chuma jutted his chin toward the station. "Some nights I see him.

Walking where church was," he said softly.

Tom smiled wistfully. "Ever since we made arrangements to come back, I've seen him — just a moment, just a glance — on a street corner, in a window... on the plane. I almost expect —" He stopped, squinted, his heart starting to pound — then he relaxed, and took a breath. "For a second, there, I thought I saw —" He stopped, shook his head. "It was just a shadow."

Chuma, couldn't translate everything but still understood, sighed and answered him. Tom turned, caught the soldier's eye and held his hands open to show that he didn't understand. "The boy says, 'Sometimes what we see in shadows is clearer than what we see by light,'" the soldier translated, and went back to directing the diggers.

"Maybe we're making a mistake," Tom said softly.

"What's that?" his brother asked.

Tom turned. "I said maybe we're making a mistake. I'm beginning to think Mark would have wanted to stay here." He paused. "And I think he would have wanted to rebuild. We did good things here, Barry. You saw. You were part of it. We did good things. It's a shame to let evil drive them out."

Barry looked away. "I knew you were going to think that."

Tom shrugged. "It's honestly what I think. You — you came back, you proved you weren't afraid to do that, but you have to go home, where they can take better care of you. But I — Mark and I — I think we belong here. The mission station has been bought by blood, now — it's not something to be thrown away."

Barry shook his head. "What are you going to tell his family — the rest of the team? How are you going to explain it to them?"

"I don't know — but I have to try." He walked over to where the soldier was standing, began to talk quietly. His brother just shook his head and leaned on his canes, looked through the trees to the burned out mission station. After a few moments he squinted and leaned forward... and wondered.

What *was* that, that he saw in the ruins?

Third Sunday of Easter

Luke 24:36-48

Ghosts (Part 3)

John Randall looked up when his daughter stopped at the threshold of the kitchen and stood for a moment, her face frozen in an uncertain expression. She said nothing at first, though her lips moved a few times as though she couldn't quite connect words to mouth. Finally, she took a deep breath, let it out slowly and said quietly, "Dad, Mom has something she wants to tell you."

It was his turn, then, to not quite form words.

"I know," his daughter said, "but she's awake. And she wants to see you."

He nodded with a quick bob of his head, stood up and followed her to the study where Margaret Randall's bed had been set up when she came home from the hospital the last time. When they walked in, she was lying perfectly still in the center of her bed, arms and hands outside the blanket, hands curled on either side of her. Her skin was sallow, her face a skeletal version of the one he still saw whenever he closed his eyes.

He stood next to the bed silently, then reached down and covered her hand with his. "It's John, Maggie. I'm here with Margaret."

Her hand twitched beneath his, and her parchment-like eyelids blinked slowly, then stayed open. Her eyes wandered around the room for a moment, then fixed on him. "John," she said softly, her voice brittle. She licked her lips. "John?"

He squeezed her hand. "Right here, Maggie."

"John." Pause. "I *saw* him, John."

"Saw who, dear?"

"Mark."

It was a breath, a quick exhalation, just barely a word, and if it hadn't been for the expression on their daughter's face, John could have convinced himself that he'd misheard it. He squeezed his wife's hand again, said gently, "Maggie, you know Mark is —"

"Mark is *here*," she said, her voice surprisingly strong. "He was here. In the chair next to me. He held my hand and said my name." She trailed off, was silent for a bit, then lifted her chin and said, "He told me not to worry. That I would be okay." She paused again, and her eyes took on a far-away look. "He said he wanted to stay in Kufasi. That his heart was there. So much to watch. So much to see." She trailed off again, closed her eyes.

When he thought she had drifted off, she added with her eyes closed, "He hoped I would understand."

To hear her speak with such certainty — with a forcefulness that had not been a part of her being for weeks, if not months — made John's spine tingle. He licked his lips, said quietly, "Maggie?" Pause. Slightly louder, "Maggie?" When there was no response, he patted her hand and straightened up; he glanced at the IV bag, now almost empty, and said wistfully, "I'm grateful that Doctor Haslip is able to keep her pain-free. But I wish..." He let the thought go, not willing to say it, for it was a selfish thing to wish that another would be conscious and aware even at death's door. *Better she should slip away in a dream*, he thought.

"You think she was just hallucinating, Dad?" Margaret asked.

He shrugged. "Morphine will do that. I remember from the war," he added.

They stood in silence, then, listening to her raspy breathing, looking down at the woman they could barely recognize. After what seemed like a very long time, his daughter said, "There's just one thing, Dad." When he looked at her and raised an eyebrow, she added, "I didn't take any morphine — and I saw him, too. As real as you or me — just like I'm seeing you now."

#

John Randall sat at the coffee table, head down, eyes fixed on nothing, trying to decide if he was dreaming. The linoleum beneath his feet was cold; his eyes itched; the coffee mug around which he'd wrapped both hands was hot — almost too hot to hold. Outside, over the humming of the icemaker, he could hear the morning birds greeting one another as

Third Sunday of Easter

they started a new day.

If this was a dream, it was a remarkably detailed one.

The kitchen phone rang, then, and seemed out of place — it rang several more times before he convinced himself to get up and answer it. By then, Margaret had come from the study to answer it, but stopped when she heard him pick it up, and stood waiting in the hallway, out of sight while she listened to one side of the conversation.

"This is Pastor John." There was a long pause.

"Brown? Tom Brown?" She could almost hear him smile. "Good morning, Doctor Brown. No, no don't be silly, I've been up —" He looked at his watch. "— since Thursday. What time is it in Kufasi? Almost one?"

There was another long pause.

"No, no, I understand — I can't believe you were even able to get a phone call out." He shuffled back to the table with the receiver, took a sip of coffee while he listened, then nodded. "I'm glad the security forces have been so helpful. Were you able to locate… our son?"

Another sip… then another. And then he sat down, put his elbow on the table and held his head with his free hand.

"Tom," he said slowly, "I've always known you to be a reasonable man — if that's what you think you saw, then… No, I don't believe in ghosts, either. But I believe in miracles." Pause. "Maybe that *would* be for the best, then. Call me when you get back — I'll help you get the wheels turning, here, to rebuild the mission station."

There were goodbyes, then he hung up the call, and got up to put the receiver back on the wall. He saw Margaret, then, standing in the hallway, and shook his head. "I'm sorry, Mags. Your brother — Mark — he's staying in Kufasi. Tom Brown said they went to M'Batha this morning, and while they were there he —" Tom hesitated, then just said it outright. "— he *saw* your brother. What he *thinks* was your brother. And then he knew what he had to do. They're going to rebuild the mission, open it up again."

His daughter said nothing, at first, then stepped up to him and put her arms around him, hugged him tightly and buried her face in his shoulder. "It's just that he's so far from home, Dad. So far," she said, her voice muffled.

He patted her back, said gently, "I know. But home is where the heart is, and his heart is with the people in M'Batha. He wanted to help them so much… I think this is his way — *God's* way — of letting us know that a little thing like death can't stop God's love."

She lifted her face, then, and stood back, looked him in the eye. "So tell me — *did* Mom and I see a ghost? His ghost?"

John smiled and said, "Let me tell you what I told your brother Mark, a long time ago. I believe once in a while — if the reason is good enough — God will let this world and the next touch, long enough to open a window. Call it a ghost, if you want — I'll just call it a miracle." He took her hand in his and squeezed it. "Now, let me go sit with your mother for a while, and tell her the good news."

Fourth Sunday of Easter

John 10:11-18

Listen

George Mason Randall hunched his shoulders and looked up automatically at the sizzle that split the air, rising to a crescendo, then fading, finally ending in a *crump!* that punctuated its short journey. He couldn't help it — even after a week, the sound of artillery overhead seemed to grab him by the gut and shake him. In a world where no one else bothered to look up, it marked him as a rookie — a fresh faced recruit still shaking the dirt of the family farm off his boots, a replacement who might become a real soldier if he lived long enough... and learned to control his reflexes.

As if to show contrition, he took his eyes off the sky and looked down. The mud — it was best to think of it as mud, instead of the stew of dirt, dead rats, and garbage it really was — was drying out, barely covering the tops of his boots. Even so it was still thick, like the remnant of hell's molasses stuck in the bottom of a bucket; the walk from the squad dugout to the observation post was a labor in itself.

"You scared, Randall?"

Lost in his thoughts, it took being repeated for the question to penetrate. He raised his eyes, saw Sergeant Du Champ staring at him, barely visible in the predawn light. "Beg pardon?" he asked.

"I said, 'are you scared?'" Du Champ pulled a pack of Camels out of his pocket, tapped one out, offered the pack to Randall, who turned it down. The sergeant put the cigarette in his mouth and struck a match, cupped it with both hands to keep the flame from being seen while he lit the cigarette. In the trench, it was a useless gesture, but anywhere else it would help keep him alive. Seventeen months of sudden death around him had taught him that *every* action he took should be taken with survival in mind; it only took one thoughtless slip to invite some Hun to put a bullet through his head.

Randall briefly considered answering the question honestly, then pushed the impulse aside and lied. "No, Sergeant."

Du Champ took a deep drag from his cigarette, let the smoke drift out of his mouth toward Randall. "That's too bad. Bein' scared is what's going to keep you alive out there."

"Last week you said following orders would keep me alive."

Du Champ grinned, his teeth visible in the half-light. "I lied. Following orders *will* keep you doing what you're s'posed to be doing but being scared will keep you alive. The trick is to learn to do both." Another drag, another slow exhalation. "Here's the thing, farmboy — we lose people all the time, even when we're not fighting. Just in the day-to-day skirmishes and artillery fire that happens for no reason other than because God gave us gunpowder and dynamite, there's upwards of five thousand men a day killed and wounded along the front. What do you s'pose happens when the brass order us to go over the top?" Du Champ paused, then mimed a machine gunner firing his weapon and spit softly, "Rat-tat-tat-tat-tat-tat…"

Randall swallowed hard, blinked, then stared.

Du Champ looked him in the eye and said, "Once you poke your head up and climb over the top… once you start across no-man's land… your odds of living out the day are crap. You can get shot up, blown up, or gassed — and if the Huns don't do it to you, your own people might, just because in the thick of battle it happens that way. Don't believe me? A gun crew shooting a twelve inch gun from ten miles away only has to make a one percent error to drop a quarter-ton of explosives on your head. You understand?"

From somewhere inside, then, Randall summoned up a grunt and said, "Geez, Sergeant, there's no need to pretty it up for me."

The sergeant grinned again, nodded slightly in approval. "Okay, then. So that's where we are. Once you get up there —" he jerked his thumb toward the land beyond the parapet — "the whole world is trying to kill you. You have to remember that and be scared of *everything*. Question everything. Trust nothing." He paused. "Almost nothing."

"*Almost* nothing, Sergeant?"

Sergeant Du Champ unbuttoned the top button of his wool tunic and reached inside, pulled out what looked to be a small cylinder hooked to a chain around his neck.

"You trust me, and you trust this," he said, holding up the brass colored object. "Out there, it's chaos — chances are you won't even be able to *see* whoever's leading the charge, let alone hear them. So you listen for *this*, instead."

Randall leaned forward, squinting a little. "Is that a whistle, Sergeant?"

"It is. And for you, it's your lifeline. It's going to tell you what to do, and when. When you hear one long note, it means you attack forward." He put the whistle to his lips, blew a very soft, long note, barely audible against the background noise of the artillery barrage that had been going on for three hours. "Three shorts, you stop and take cover." Three short, soft notes. "Two longs, you drop what you're doing and rally on me — you follow the whistle." Two long, soft notes. "And two shorts and a long mean you follow me and pull back to our lines." Two short and one long, soft notes. Du Champ eyed him closely. "You got it?"

Randall's head bobbed.

"You do *whatever* the whistle says, right? Because that's going to be me." He tucked the whistle in the front pocket of his tunic. "Farm boy, I've got a wife, a girlfriend, and three kids back home, and I aim to see every one of them again. I am going to live through this godforsaken war, and my aim is to do it with as many of you boys as I can, if you'll let me. So for God's sake, trust me. Trust what I'm calling you to do. You know my whistle, and you listen, and we're all going to get home when this is over. Got it?"

Randall swallowed hard, again, and nodded. "If it means getting home to Ma again, I'll follow you anywhere."

"And I will get you there, if it's the last thing I do." There was a sudden silence, then, as the barrage stopped. Du Champ looked up for the first time, at the fading stars, then he pulled out his pocket watch and opened it, glanced and snapped it shut. "It's ten minutes to six, Farm Boy. We'd best get the squad up if we're going to meet our maker on time. The colonel is a stickler for punctuality." With that, he strode back toward the dugout, ready to rouse his men... and lead them.

And in the days and weeks to come, Randall would be amazed at how well he could hear the whistle through the apocalyptic chaos, and how comforting it was to have something to guide him… as long as he remembered to listen.

Fifth Sunday of Easter

John 15:1-8

Vines And Spines

"So, who do you think he's going to be today?" Thomas asked quietly, as he sorted through clothing, just peering at some in the gloom and giving the sniff test to others. A few of the latter he tossed into a pile in the corner. "Is Martha doing laundry today, I hope?" he added.

"Probably," Mary answered, tidying the other side of the room — then she stopped and looked at him. "Of course, if she doesn't, you could always do it."

Thomas stopped, looked at her and tilted his head.

"Right. That's just crazy talk," Mary murmured, then raised her voice. "What do you mean, who do I think he's going to be?"

"The shepherd, the fisherman, the farmer —"

Mary nodded. "Got it."

"— the arborist, the carpenter, the vineyard laborer —"

"Got it," Mary repeated.

"I mean, he's our *rabbi* — why doesn't he just *teach*? Would it kill him to just answer a question directly once in a while? Or just tell us something, straight out? Instead we get metaphors, like 'I am the true vine, and my father is the gardener.'" He finished sorting, then, wiped his hands on his tunic and looked at the pile of laundry. "I hope your sister does laundry. It's really piling up."

"That's really more of an allegory, not a metaphor," Mary said quietly.

"There's nothing allegorical about dirty laundry."

"Don't be so sure. But I meant what the Master said about being the true vine. It's an allegory. You got that, right?"

"Of course!" Thomas blustered, then shrugged. "But why can't he just say what he means? Or talk about something I know? I'm a fisherman — talk to me about fish. Better yet, just say what he means — I'm a simple man."

Mary smiled. "You and the others are anything but simple. Thick headed, sometimes, but you're not simple."

Thomas looked at his hostess closely, then shrugged. "Thank you?"

"You're welcome." She hesitated, then extended her hand in invitation and said, "Come with me, Thomas."

"Where?"

"Just come with me."

He followed her out of the house, where she stopped just outside the door, before the gate that led out onto the road through town. She looked around on the ground, picked up a stick, and began drawing in the dust. Drawing quickly, she sketched out a very simple fish skeleton, tapped it with the end of the stick and looked at Thomas. "What's this?"

Thomas studied the drawing, gave a small shrug this time. "Tilapia, I think."

"No — well, okay, but I meant what's *this*?" She tapped the sketch again, directly on a thick line that ran from the fish's head to its tail.

"Oh — that's the fish's spine. The backbone."

"Right. And what are these?" The tip of the stick moved to lines radiating off the spine.

"Fish bones. Don't know that they have a name."

"Right. And what do all these do, together?"

"They provide the shape for the fish — they hold the guts they make a framework so the fish can move. They form the structure for the fish. They make it possible for the fish to swim — to move."

"Okay." She paused, then used the stick to brush away dust, creating a gap partway down the spine. "If the spine breaks, can the fish move?"

Thomas hesitated, then shook his head. "No — not past where it breaks, anyway. That part of the fish would just hang there — it really wouldn't be able to move like it was supposed to."

She used the stick to create gaps between some of the bones and the spine. "What about this — if the bones break from the spine?"

"Same thing. It wouldn't work the way it's supposed to. Maybe it couldn't swim at all, maybe it would just flounder. The fish could maybe lose one or two, but not many."

"Right. Right." She looked down at the fish skeleton and nodded to herself, then looked back to Thomas and pointed to the sketch with the stick. "This is you — all of you — and Jesus. All of his followers, and Jesus," Mary amended, silently adding herself and other women she knew to the list. "Jesus is the spine, the backbone — without him, nothing else is possible. Every other follower is like one of these bones, here, coming off the spine — like a rib, or whatever you call it. As long as you're taking direction from the spine — from Jesus — the fish is swimming and doing its fish thing. But if you break off from the spine — then you're not contributing to the life of the fish. Break off enough, and the fish will flounder completely. But as long as you remain attached — faithful — to the spine, and the spine remains attached to you, it thrives. Does that make sense?"

Thomas looked down at the sketch and nodded slowly. "Yeah, that makes a lot of sense." He was silent for a bit, then looked back up to Mary. "Why didn't he just say *that*?"

Mary smiled. "Maybe you should ask him — but don't be surprised if you don't get a straight answer."

Thomas smiled back, in spite of himself. "Yeah — I don't doubt that."

Sixth Sunday of Easter

John 15:9-17

An Act Of Love

Mademoiselle from Armentieres,

Parlez-vous

Mademoiselle from Armentieres,

Parlez-vous

I didn't much care what came of me,

So I went and joined the infantry

Hinky-dinky parlez-vous. (in the public domain)

"Ain't that the truth," George Randall murmured in answer to the song going through his head. The song, with its seemingly infinite number of verses, had been shouldering its way into his thoughts most of the afternoon — a way for his brain to divert his attention from the very real possibility of being blown up, bayoneted, shot, or gassed between one heartbeat and the next.

    He lay back against the crater wall, where he had just slid down from the rim, and scanned the place where he had come to rest, whistled softly at what he saw. Going over the top and trying to force a passage across no man's land, he had focused on avoiding the moonlike craters that dominated the landscape; now that he was in one he could truly appreciate how big it was. The first house he could remember, back when his mother was still living on the Lac des Mortes reservation, would have fit easily in this one, with room to spare. Through the dust and gloom, he picked out several other men sharing the space — three almost directly across from him, one other just to his right, sprawled on the floor of the crater.

Well, *part* of one, he amended after a closer look, then closed his eyes and rested his head on the crater wall.

Mademoiselle from Armentieres,

Parlez-vous…

He sighed, opened his eyes and looked toward the three men across the crater, waved to them and started over, keeping to the wall of the crater. It was instinctive — and useless; the Germans couldn't possibly see him, as deep as the crater was, and if an artillery round happened to fall into the crater, it wouldn't much matter where he was. Even so, it just *felt* safer.

"Hey farmboy," a familiar voice called out as he got closer, and it took him a moment to recognize it — not just because of the ringing in his ears, but because the voice itself was softer. "You're a sight for sore eyes," the voice added, "I figured you to be hangin' on the wire out there."

"No sir, Sergeant Du Champ," George answered, now directly in front of his sergeant, who was sitting next to two men — a kid named Gottschalk, from his squad, and one that George didn't recognize. The one he didn't recognize had a bandage around his head, covering his eyes. He looked back at Du Champ. "I heard your whistle, when we got bogged down out there — you called us back."

"Not fast enough," Du Champ said, even more quietly. "I don't think many of us are left. Gottschalk was hung up in the wire when I found him —" the private just stared at him vacantly, then looked away. "— and Willy, here —" he nudged the bandaged soldier — "is from Able Company, about a mile down the line from us. Found him in no man's land."

"Did he take some gas in the eyes?" George guessed — he couldn't see well enough to know if there was blistering.

"No, the bandage is just sorta holding in his eyeballs 'til the docs can look at him," Du Champ explained. "He was too close to a round that dropped when the Huns started shelling us the second time. The concussion blew out his ears and popped out his eyeballs. When I found him, he was trying to push 'em back in. Did the best I could and bandaged him up. Don't know if he'll be blind or not." He paused, flashed the smile George was familiar with — and for no reason, George started to believe things were going to be all right. "So we've been sitting here, wondering how we were going to make it back to the line, and then who shows up — farmboy. Like I said, you're a sight for sore eyes."

"So what's the plan?"

"What makes you think I have a plan?" Du Champ asked.

"You *always* have a plan," George answered. "You told me once that I should always have at least two plans: a plan to kill every Hun I meet, and a plan to make it back to the line in one piece from wherever I am." He paused, then chuckled. "And then you said *those* plans were subject to whatever *your* plans were, because the first plan any of us were supposed to have was to follow you."

Du Champ nodded. "That does sound like something I would say. And I *do* have a plan, as a matter of fact." He took out his watch, opened it. "In about ten minutes, our artillery batteries are going to start pouring it on — that's part of the operation." He looked up, toward the rim of the crater. "And it's dark enough, now, that when the artillery starts up, we can make our move. Single file, up over the top right *there* —" he pointed to a particular spot on the rim, and after about a hundred yard run, we'll be right at the forward trench. You take the lead, with Willy hanging onto your belt, and Gottschalk hanging on to Willy's, and me bringing up the rear. If we don't stop to smell the roses, we'll be back there in no time. Sound like a plan, farmboy?"

"How fast can a blind man run over broken ground?" George asked doubtfully.

"Not as fast as you, but fast enough. And we sure as hell can't leave anyone behind, so…" the sergeant trailed off.

George nodded, shrugged. "I knew you'd have a plan, Sergeant. I just hope the Huns aren't watching us."

"They'll be too busy keeping their heads down — *and* it will be dark."

The latter was definitely true; it was already almost too dark to see the rim of the crater. The battlefield had become eerily quiet, with only the occasional *wheet!* of a bullet cracking overhead, and the cries of the wounded on every side as they poured out their fear and pain as sound, an atonal symphony of the dying. As George tried to imagine what it would be like to be lying out there, gut-shot and waiting to die — then tried to push that image away — another thought occurred to him. He leaned toward Du Champ and said quietly, "I know it's going to be dark, and all — but did you give any thought to us just *crawling* back to the line?"

Equally quietly, the sergeant said, "On a good night, leading a blind soldier and a victim of shellshock, it might take an hour to crawl that far. I don't think I have that much time."

George grinned. "Got a hot date, Sarge?"

Mademoiselle from Armentieres,

parlez vous…

Du Champ grunted. "Sure — with a doctor. I took a bullet in my right lung about an hour ago, through and through, and it bleeds like a son of a gun anytime I move. *And* I can't catch my breath."

"Geez, Sarge — why don't I just go out and find a medic for you?"

Another grunt, and a wheeze. "No chance, farmboy. It's my job to get you boys back to the line. Even Willy, there — it's what I have to do." He looked down at his watch, watched the secondhand traverse from one glowing number to the next. After a moment or two he closed the face of it and put it in his pocket. "Should be any time, now."

Almost as though they had been waiting on his pronouncement, artillery shells began to sizzle overhead, falling on the German lines a couple of hundred yards ahead.

Wordlessly, he tapped George on the shoulder to get him to his feet, then pulled Willy to his feet and guided his hand to George's belt. "When I whistle, you go — up and out, and toward our lines. Got it?" He repeated the instructions, yelling them directly into Willy's ear. In any other context, it would have been funny… but not here, not now.

Slowly, conscious of the hand at his back, and the soldier behind *him*, and the sergeant behind *them*, he walked to the spot Du Champ had pointed out and began to climb. Fortunately, it was a shallow grade, and when he got to the top edge he stopped, waited. The sound of artillery was fierce, now, and he thought for the thousandth time that this was what angels must hear when they flew inside a thunder cloud.

After what seemed like an eternity — maybe all of thirty seconds — he heard Du Champ's whistle: three long blasts. Without conscious thought, he scrambled over the top and crouched, reached back awkwardly to help Willy, who turned to pull Gottschalk out of the crater; Du Champ was right behind, and by starlight George could see the sergeant motioning for him to move. He took a bearing on a branchless tree that he knew was near their section of trench and began to move toward it. It couldn't properly be called running, given the churned ground and the tug on his belt reminding him he was leading two men — one blind, the other addled. Sergeant Du Champ was not a concern — he could handle himself.

He had not taken more than a handful of steps when one of those shells screamed overhead from the direction of the German lines, and burst behind their own lines — a brilliant flash that sent stars shooting into the sky and seemed to burn like a tiny sun, illuminating the American lines in silhouette... and he stood frozen, rooted in place, aware with every cell of his being that they were clear targets, now, and utterly convinced that there was no point in running, no point in moving, even, because in the next instant he — they — would be cut in half by German machine guns.

He remembered thinking, it would be ridiculous to die running...

Three blasts of the whistle cut through his paralysis, and in the next moment he heard a wild yell from behind, turned to see Sergeant Du Champ roaring at the top of his lungs as he ran full speed in the opposite direction, firing his pistol toward the German trenches. On the run, with his other hand he hurled a grenade in that direction, doing nothing but sending out a flash and a cloud of dust. In approximately the same moment, German slugs began kicking up dirt as their gunners walked the streams of lead on target with deadly precision.

George ran as fast as he could, reaching back to drag Willy along as he ran toward their trench, looking back once to make sure Gottschalk was still there. They did not stop when he reached the edge of the trench but threw himself into it; Willy tumbled after him, and Gottschalk jumped awkwardly. When he got his breath back, and had shoved Willy off, he scrambled to his feet. There was a fusillade of fire, now, from his own trench as others answered the German machine guns.

George had the presence of mind to find a medic for Willy, and to send Gottschalk along with him, before unslinging his own rifle… but by then the fire had dwindled, then stopped. Carefully, he mounted the parapet and poked his head above the trench, peered out in the direction they had come… but there was no one there. As he stared into the empty darkness, then, he wondered…

Had this been Du Champ's plan all along — to lay down his life for his men?

What kind of man would do such a thing, he wondered?

And in the silence of the battlefield he heard something his mother had read to him, once: "Greater love hath no man than this, that he lay down his life for his friends…"

"Dammit, Sarge, I wish you'd've told me your plan," he whispered in the darkness, "At least I could have said goodbye."

Ascension of the Lord

Luke 24:44-53

Anticipation

Thomas closed the shutter, plunging the room into shadow, and sat down heavily on a stool in front of the window. He closed his eyes and gently bumped his head against the wooden shutter a couple of times, opened them and looked around the room. Shadows were cast against the walls, flickering in time with the oil lamps that cast their indifferent light. On the far side of the shutter, noise from the street reminded him that there was a life out there — ; people talking loudly and laughing, donkeys braying, children chattering.

He bounced his head against the shutter again, a little harder this time.

"You're going to break it," Mary cautioned, as she straightened things that didn't need straightening. "The shutter, I mean — I'm pretty sure your head's too thick to break," she added.

"Ha. Ha. Ha. You're funny. You and your brother should go on tour — the Laz and Mary Show."

She smiled. "You have to admit, my brother putting on a shroud and shuffling into your room last night was pretty funny."

"If it was so funny, why wasn't I laughing?"

"Because you have a sour disposition and no sense of humor?" Mary guessed.

"There's nothing funny about being stuck here... waiting."

"Why didn't you go to the temple with the others? They've gone every day, and you just sit around the house, like you're trying to turn moping into a high art."

"Why don't I go? You heard Jesus: 'Wait in the city until you have been clothed in power.' So I'm waiting in the city until he sends whoever or whatever it is that's going to do all these things for us. I don't want to be off at the temple when he shows up. I'm not going to take a chance on missing him — or it. Or whatever is going to clothe us in glory. I missed

Ascension of the Lord

the Master coming back, once — I'm not going to have that happen again." He rolled his eyes. "But I'm *sooo* bored!"

"Maybe you need to do something."

"Like what?"

"I don't know." Mary looked around. "Clean, maybe?"

Thomas looked at her, shook his head. "Let's just say, for the sake of argument, I did that — then what would *you* do?"

Mary looked thoughtful. "I don't know, Thomas — maybe go to temple with the others?"

"You too?"

"Of course, me too. I — we — Martha and I — are just as joyful as you are. Or as you should be, anyway. The Master came back to us, Thomas, how can you not feel joy at that?"

"I feel plenty of joy — I'm practically *oozing* joy from every pore. Yes, the Master came back — and then he went away. Again. He left us. Again. Jesus rose *from the dead*, Mary. Maybe having a brother who's done the same thing has made you a little jaded, but —" He shrugged. "I don't get it. At Passover we ran like frightened children, and left him to die. A few days later he rose from the dead and came back to us as though nothing happened. Treated us like old friends, then he told us that *we* would go forth and spread his teachings — his gospel — to all the world. And before any of us could ask how that was going to happen, he left. Just up and left. So pardon me if I feel more confused than joyful." He shook his head.

Mary nodded. "Okay, I get that. Believe me, I can relate to confusion. It's why I've spent so much time listening and talking to Jesus, asking him to repeat things, trying to understand exactly what he meant when he said so many of the things he said. There is very little of what we've learned from him that was easy — but now that he's opened our minds, we can look back and see where we've been wrong, or thickheaded... or both. Surely you can see that, can't you?"

"I see it just fine. Just as well as I see us — well, *me* — letting him down. When the most spectacular, amazing, incredible thing happened, and he came back to show us he had risen, I wasn't there. And I didn't believe. Not until I saw him standing here — almost right here, in this very spot. Then when I finally wrapped my head around the idea of Jesus being back among us, he dropped that final lesson on us, and left. Back to heaven." He folded his arms, wrapping his tunic a little more tightly around himself, and scowled. "He said wait, stay — so I'm not moving until something happens."

Mary was silent for a bit, just watching him, then she crossed the room and started to kneel next to him — stopped, pulled up another stool, and *sat* next to him. He eyed her while she reached out and put her hand on his folded arms, then wriggled her fingers until he let her hand slip between them so she could grasp one of his hands. "Thomas — friend. Don't you see, something *has* happened, already. When Jesus was here, teaching us, we struggled — we *all* struggled so hard to understand, and more often than not we missed the mark. And then he died, and came back to us when no one expected it, and in the joy of getting him back he opened up our minds so we could understand it all. The law, his teachings, how so many things the prophets said pointed directly to our Master, and what happened to him — we suddenly could understand it all. Right?"

Thomas nodded grudgingly.

"And now we also understand that he's tasked us with sharing the good news of his presence with the rest of the world — taking his love to the corners of the earth. Right?"

"Right," he grunted.

"You are one of a handful of people who have seen and talked to the Son of God — the Messiah — who've had the chance to sit at his feet and learn from him. And you've witnessed his resurrection. Right?"

He didn't answer, so she squeezed his hand. "Right?"

"Right," he agreed.

"Then don't sit there like a petulant little boy and tell me you're going to wait for something to happen. Something *has* happened. You've seen miracle upon miracle, sign upon sign — you've walked with Jesus from Galilee to Jerusalem, from life to death, and back to life again. Things have happened, and you've been in the thick of them. I hardly believe that if you go to temple to celebrate all that, that God would overlook you now."

Thomas looked at her then, and smiled faintly. "Do you really think so?"

She nodded, squeezed his hand.

There was a short pause, then Thomas stood up; Mary's hand fell away, and she stood up as well. "If that's the case," Thomas said, "then I suppose we ought to go to the temple. There is much to be thankful for."

They left for the temple together, and neither noticed that the wind seemed to be picking up....

Seventh Sunday of Easter

John 17:6-19

Mysterious Ways

"Mind if I ask you a question, Reverend Lee?"

Jamison Lee turned to him, hymnals in hand, and nodded. "As long as you go easy on me, Sergeant Wayne. The baby's been teething, and she hasn't slept through the night for a week."

Eustice Wayne paused, then said, "Whiskey, sir — have you tried whiskey?"

Jamison tapped his clergy collar with the tip of his finger. "Frowned upon, Sergeant."

"Not for you, sir, beggin' your pardon. But if you put a bit of whiskey on the tip of your finger and rub it on your little girl's gums, she'll be good as gold, sir. My missus and I used it on all five of ours."

Jamison raised an eyebrow. "You have five children, Sergeant? I had no idea."

With barely a pause, Eustice Wayne answered, "*Had*, sir — we *had* five. Cholera took one of the boys while we were in Missouri, and consumption took two of the girls when we were in Nebraska. But my oldest is married to a farmer, with a girl of her own, and my son is — well, he should be at Fort Lincoln, by now." Wayne couldn't resist a grin. "He's a lieutenant, freshly minted from the Academy, assigned to the Cavalry."

Jamison shifted the books in his hands, reached out and shook Wayne's hand. "Well, congratulations, Sergeant. I know you're very proud."

"I am, Reverend Lee. He's a good boy, he'll go far in this man's Army. And bein' an officer, he won't have to work very hard, either."

Jamison smiled. "Spoken like a true enlisted man."

"Yes, sir. Now my question — if you don't mind my askin' — why do you think Jesus let his men off the hook the way he did? Last time you were here at the fort, you talked about how they all ran off when Jesus got arrested — Peter even lied about not knowing him. And yet when Jesus rose up and came back to them, everything was hunky-dory."

"That's true," Jamison agreed.

"Well — no offense to the saints, reverend, but those men were cowardly, and there'd be no putting up with that in my book. We had a man — a captain, he was, last name of Connors. He led his troops into a trap, and then ran away when the hostiles attacked. They drummed him out of the Army — stripped him of everything, right there in front of us. Far as I know, he just disappeared into the wilderness with nothin' but a guilty conscience. You probably saw similar things, sir, during the War?"

Jamison nodded slowly. "I did, Sergeant. Saw a few men hanged — not from my regiment. Cowardice is one of the Army's deadly sins, and they will not put up with it. I suppose," he said thoughtfully, "it's a good thing the disciples weren't in the Army."

"True enough, but they're in God's army, sort of — weren't they?"

"I suppose they were." Jamison paused. "There's a couple of ways to look at it, Sergeant. The conventional explanation is that Jesus is just that forgiving — after all, he forgave the men who nailed him to the cross. And he forgave the thief who asked for his mercy. By dying up there on the cross, Jesus made it possible for *everyone* to be forgiven, even cowards. And by forgiving his disciples, he was just living out the grace and forgiveness that he preached. After all, they *were* scared — nobody expected things to happen the way they did, except maybe Jesus himself."

Wayne nodded, taking it in, then said, "You said there was another way to look at it, reverend?"

Jamison hesitated. "Well, this is just me, mind you. But as a career soldier, you might appreciate it, too. Remember how, in today's gospel reading, John tells us that Jesus was praying for his disciples? Basically, he was telling God that they'd learned everything he could teach them, so now he was putting them back in God's hands? He says something like, 'The world hates them... my prayer is that you will protect them.' Then he says he's sending them into the world, and he asks God to watch over them,"

Lectionary Stories for Preaching and Teaching

The sergeant nodded again. "I remember."

"Well — ten or fifteen years ago, when I was *Colonel* Lee, I sent men on missions or into battle against pretty tall odds, sometimes. Had to. But most of the time, the last line in my written orders was the same: 'If it looks as though you can't accomplish the mission or be victorious, you are authorized to withdraw and fight another day.'" He paused. "I saw too many men slaughtered on the battlefield when there was no chance of victory, just wasted, to ever want to be a party to it if I didn't have to be."

He looked somber. "Sometimes, withdrawal just is not an option — and I expected my officers to recognize those occasions, too. We who've fought for our country know that sometimes dying gallantly is a necessity. But I didn't believe in sending my men to die for no reason."

After a moment, "I'm sure your men appreciated that, sir."

"I'd like to think so — but even so, we managed to bury a lot of brave men down there, sergeant. Too many. So that makes me wonder if, maybe, God *did* protect the disciples — not with big, flashy miracles like lightning from the sky that smote their enemies, but by giving them enough sense to run when there was no point in fighting. The Romans were the finest soldiers of the day — and even a squad of legionaries grown fat on garrison duty would have been enough to annihilate the disciples, if they'd fought back in Gethsemane. Where would we be then? Surviving to tell the story — surviving to witness the resurrection, to spread the gospel — *that* is a lot more meaningful then getting gutted by a sword, or nailed to the cross next to Jesus', isn't it?"

"So... God made them cowards? And that's why Jesus didn't mind?"

"I like to think of it as God giving them common sense in the face of overwhelming odds — and Jesus understood that... or at least trusted that his Father did what he'd asked him to do." He shrugged. "Think about it, Sergeant Wayne — most of these men were fishermen. They were physically tough, and I'm guessing Peter wasn't the only one who wasn't inclined to back down from a fight. It could have been a massacre, there in Gethsemane — men killing and being killed over the Prince of Peace. But it wasn't — so instead of a dozen dead martyrs, we have the gospels, and a legacy of faith."

Sergeant Wayne considered the explanation and nodded. "That makes sense, reverend — and it changes how I think of them. You've given me a lot to think about."

Jamison Lee chuckled. "That's what I'm here for, Sergeant — to make you think. Now, if you could help me get these on the shelves, so I can find them when we come back to Fort Bellah next month…" He held out a stack of books and the two old soldiers continued to talk as they shelved Bibles and hymnals.

Day of Pentecost

John 15:26-27; 16:4b-15

The Draft, The Advocate, And Paul Hornung

"Why do you suppose he had to leave?"

John Randall barely hesitated as he wiped stain onto the edge of a bookshelf. "Well — it's complicated, but every team in the league had to put up players in what they call the expansion draft, so the new team in New Orleans can have their pick of some veteran football players. Otherwise they would just get stuck with new players coming out of college, and they wouldn't be able to compete with the other teams. For Green Bay, this year, it just made sense to take a chance putting Paul Hornung into the draft. And he's great, so the Saints took him." He dipped his rag in the can of stain, looked at his son. "We hated to see him go."

Mark looked puzzled. "No, Dad. I wasn't talking about Paul Hornung."

His father was silent for a moment, reviewing their conversation while he began staining the rest of the shelf. "We were just talking about the Packers, weren't we?" he asked finally. "Or have the fumes gotten to me?"

"No, no," Mark protested, then stepped back. "Well, yes, we were, but we're done with them now. I was thinking about your sermon today — about how Jesus was telling his disciples he was going to leave them, and they were going to miss him, but that someone else —"

"The Advocate. The Holy Spirit," John put in.

"— yeah, that guy, was going to come and tell them things. But I was just thinking, if Jesus knew his guys were going to miss him, why couldn't he just stay? I mean, he knew he was going to die, but he also knew it wasn't going to last, right? So when he came back, he could have just stayed."

"Interesting way to put it, but you're right, he *did* die and it *didn't* last. He came back."

"So why not just stick around — you know, maybe forever? Wouldn't it be cool to have Jesus here, now? I mean, there's stuff that we're stuck figuring out from the Bible that would be a whole lot easier if we could just ask him, right?"

Hey Jesus, what do you think about Vietnam? John thought. *How about busing?* "I suppose it would be," he agreed cautiously.

"It's like when I ask you if something is okay and you don't know, you tell me to ask Mom —"

"That's not exactly —"

"— so wouldn't it be cool to be able to say, 'You know, that's a good question. Why don't you ask Jesus?'"

"No doubt," John agreed, "but I'm afraid that would probably be a pretty long line to stand in. Fortunately, we've got a pretty good idea of what he would think about most things, I think, we should just listen to the Holy Spirit and take the trouble to look at what he said, and the context he said it in. God gave us pretty good brains, when we care to use them."

"Not like those guys in Washington, right?"

John smiled. "Right. So your bigger question is why did Jesus leave his disciples in the first place, right?"

"Yeah. They were on a real roller coaster, weren't they?"

"They were. And Jesus leaving was going to be a really sad thing for them, since they would have to go through him being executed and buried, and then coming back after they thought they'd lost him forever." He paused, refolded the cloth, dipped it in the can again. "But remember what he said — in order for the Advocate to come, he would have to leave. And the Advocate had to come to inspire the disciples — to open their minds to everything he'd been saying, to send them out to the world, and be able to speak to people about Jesus. Without the coming of the Holy Spirit, which would happen at the Feast of Pentecost, there would be no church."

Mark looked at him thoughtfully.

"Okay, I know that look. What are you thinking?"

"Just — with no church, does that mean we wouldn't have to get up at seven in the morning on Sunday? Or sit through Sunday School?"

"Interesting way to look at it. Very narrow, but interesting. And, no, it doesn't mean that. It means millions — billions — of people around the world might never hear of Jesus Christ, or know that he came and died for them. It means they would all be lost. And if it's any comfort to you, Mom and I would still get you up at seven, just out of spite."

"But that's my question, then — if we had Jesus, we wouldn't need the church, right? I mean, it would be really different at least. Maybe he would have his own TV show, and just come on once a week to tell us what to do. And then his disciples wouldn't have had to feel sad that he left."

"That's a fascinating idea. But I think part of it has to do with what we call free will — the ability of people to choose what to do. Once we've been inspired — and that word literally means to have the spirit come into us. Once we've been inspired by the Holy Spirit, then we choose whether or not to act upon it... and that ability to make the choice is part of what makes us human. And it's part of what moves us toward the kingdom of heaven — or doesn't. By directing us, but not forcing us, God is enabling us to choose love, obedience, and service."

"But what does that —"

"And if Jesus was here, looking over our shoulder, it just wouldn't be the same. I think we would be less inspired to work hard in his name, if we knew he was just here and could do it himself, if he had to. Kind of like cleaning your room — Mom or I could do it, but we think you learning to do it yourself, and getting satisfaction out of doing it well, is important to you."

He stopped staining, looked at his handiwork and nodded, set the rag aside and put the lid back on the can. He considered what he was going to say, then shrugged and continued. "And one other thing — and I'm just guessing here. Remember, Jesus was the Son of God — he *was* God, part of the Trinity. I think that to be here, in human form and away from his father — that was hard. It's hard for us, as humans, to be away from home and family, so I can't even imagine what it must be like to be away from a spiritual, perfect existence and live here, in an imperfect and sinful world."

"So maybe it was sad for them — but Jesus was looking forward to going home?"

"I think that's not unreasonable — don't you? I mean, anyone can be homesick."

Mark nodded agreement. "I think I get it. Now — tell me about that draft thing? I've got questions."

Trinity Sunday

John 3:1-17

Table Talk

"I don't get it," Maggie Randall said abruptly as she buttered a dinner roll. When all eyes at the table turned to her, she set the knife down and tore off a piece of roll, gestured with it as she spoke. "At recess today, Bonnie Burns told me she got born again over the weekend, so she was going to go to heaven, and anyone who wasn't, wouldn't. How do I get born again? Do I have to get back in Mom's stomach?"

Margaret Randall coughed once, held up her napkin to hide a smile as she dabbed at her mouth. "Of course not, dear. Once was enough."

"But I want to go to heaven."

"Of course, and you will."

"Then how do I get born again if I don't?"

"That's not exactly how it works."

"Bonnie said that's what Jesus said. Is she lying?"

"No, Jesus did say that."

"Was Jesus lying?"

Margaret sighed and looked across the table at her husband. "Do you want to step in, here, *pastor*?"

"You seem to be doing just fine," he answered, reaching for the mashed potatoes. He swallowed an exclamation when he felt a sharp pain in his shin; Margaret just looked at him innocently and took a sip of coffee. He reached down to rub his leg, then turned to their daughter. "Of course Jesus wasn't lying, and your friend wasn't either — Jesus did say that you had to be born again, when he was talking to a Pharisee named Nicodemus."

"Was Nicodemus lying?"

"Nobody was lying, Maggie. It's just that Jesus was speaking — symbolically." He saw her expression and didn't wait for the question. "You know how I sometimes tell Mom she looks like a million bucks?"

116

"Sure. You said it this weekend, when the two of you were going to the movies."

"Right." He smiled. "Do I mean she actually looks like a million dollars?"

Maggie made a face. "That would be silly — she looks like Mom."

"Right. So you know that I mean Mom looks really good. Jesus used to say things like that all the time — he used symbols to help people understand what he was getting at. Sometimes we have trouble understanding when he said that, because it was almost two thousand years ago, and what was obvious to people *then* isn't obvious to us *now*. And sometimes, he was trying to put things in terms only certain people — his closest followers — would understand."

Margaret cleared her throat; he glanced at her and saw the warning in her eyes — *you're going too deep*. "But this time, I think Jesus was just talking in symbols," he concluded, skirting around the edge of the rabbit hole.

"Did he mean we have to be babies to go to heaven?"

"Well, kind of — but not exactly." He paused, trying to remember just how much their daughter knew about the birds and the bees. With an internal shrug, he pushed on. "Before a baby is born, it spends time in the womb — in the mom's tummy, kind of. And it's really comfortable in there. All the baby has to do is just go with the flow; doesn't have to do anything, doesn't even have to think. And then, one day, the baby gets born — and it's a *hard* thing. The baby is pushed, and squished —"

Her brother, speaking with the accumulated wisdom of a thirteen-year-old, chimed in. "Maggie, you remember cousin Norman, right? How his head was pointed when he was born? That's 'cause it got *squished* that way."

Her eyes widened a little, and their mother stepped in smoothly. "Norman looked just beautiful, like any baby. That's just something that sometimes happens and it's temporary."

"Yeah, it's hardly pointed at all, anymore," Mark agreed, and fell silent when his mother shot him a look.

John stepped back in. "That's maybe not an example I would have used, but it's not bad. In a way, being born and being born again are like that, they reshape your head — and your thinking. A baby has to leave behind the comfort of where it was — and that's kind of what happens when we decide to leave behind our old lives and turn our lives to Jesus. We leave behind what's comfortable, what we've always known, and suddenly have to look at new things, in a new way, and figure out what we think about them."

Maggie considered this, then frowned. "Is *that* all? Bonnie made it sound like a big deal."

"Accepting Jesus — realizing that Jesus is your Savior, and that Jesus is your way back to being close to God, your way to forgiveness, that *is* a big deal. When someone who never knew about Jesus suddenly realizes that Jesus is their Savior, and that we want to live life the way he wants them to, that's a very special moment. But some people, like you and Mark, grow up knowing Jesus, so I don't think you'll ever have that same kind of sudden realization. A couple thousand years ago, nobody grew up knowing Jesus, so it was *always* like being born, they were pushed, they were squished by new ideas and new teachings, and then suddenly one day it all made sense. I think that's what Jesus was talking about, when he was talking to Nicodemus."

There was a silent stretch, then — both parents watching Maggie, Mark happily chewing on dinner — and then she nodded. "Okay, I think I get it. He didn't *really* mean being born again, just that believing in him would be hard, *like* being born."

"Right. And one day you're in the dark, like being in the womb, and then suddenly you're in the light — and you're with Jesus."

"Got it. Then I have another question."

John suppressed a sigh, just raised his eyebrows in invitation.

"When a mom eats food, does the baby see it come down, and then eat it again? 'Cause that would be gross."

John *did* sigh, then, and turned to Margaret. "I think I'll let Mom handle this one, since she's done it a couple of times…"

Proper 5 / Ordinary Time 10

Mark 3:20-35

What Family Is For

Hubert Morris Randall poked at dinner with his fork, pushed it from one side of the tin plate to the other, and looked up to see his brother watching him closely, with a faintly amused expression. He paused from worrying his main course to say, "Please don't take this the wrong way, little brother, but Mother believes you have lost your mind."

Mason Randall smiled and cut off a piece of meat on his own plate, popped it in his mouth before answering. "How could I possibly take offense to that, big brother?"

"I mean, literally, she thinks you've lost your mind. She sent me up here to see if I could, in clear conscience, declare you incompetent and have you returned to Chicago for treatment. By force, if necessary."

Mason started to answer, but thought better of it and sliced off another piece of meat, chewed it slowly before he spoke. He lowered his voice so they would not be overheard. "First, speaking as a member of the bar and third in my class at law school, I'm not sure about the legality of taking me into protective custody and removing me across state lines in a mental competency case, not to mention the fact that we are, having this discussion on the soil of a sovereign Indian nation while we enjoy our dinner."

He then paused, and strategically chose not to mention that both the local county sheriff *and* the old man who led the tribal police were friends of his. Instead, he added, "Secondly, I *do* appreciate your candor, big brother, and I wonder what your medical opinion would be?"

There was another pause, while his visitor moved the main course to the other side of the plate, and tentatively speared something that looked like a carrot, popped it in his mouth. He chewed it slowly, before answering carefully, "I would tell Mother that in my professional opinion that you are *not* clinically insane. You are grounded in reality, were able to correctly answer all the questions I posed to you today, and give no sign of having aural or visual hallucinations… not that you talk about, anyway."

Mason nodded with a dip of his chin, raised his tin cup in salute, and took a sip of water.

Hubert raised his own glass, tipped it toward his brother and continued. "In my *non* professional opinion, of course, you're as mad as a hatter. You have taken the twin gifts of a first-class education and a middling-intelligent mind and wasted them both. You could have been a senior partner at any law firm in Chicago by the end of the century, or you could have gone out east and been a star at some white shoe law firm in New York or Philadelphia, making money hand over fist. Instead you end up on an Indian reservation doing what? Teaching? Wiping noses and trying to teach them English?" He shook his head, and took a deep drink of water, set the cup down, only then noticing the little bugs floating in it.

He sighed. "I know you mean well, Mason, but honestly — these are a degenerate people. Look at all the resources they've been sitting on top of for thousands of years, and they've done what with them? Nothing, until we came along. They are physically frail, susceptible to all sorts of diseases, and possibly mentally subnormal as well. You're wasting your time. You're an intelligent man, you *know* this, deep down inside — but you let your judgment get clouded by a pretty smile and some blonde hair."

For the first time since they sat down to dinner, Mason frowned. "I'm going to give you a chance to take that back, if you want to remain my brother. It's insulting to me, to my wife, and to our people, here."

"They're not *your* people, Mason —"

"They work with us and they take care of us. They trust us with their children. They worship with us on Sunday, and they rejoice with us when we're happy, they mourn with us when we're sad. They have embraced us for what we're trying to do, here, and they've never been anything but graceful and welcoming despite everything that *our* race has done to them. They take us for who we are here —" he touched his chest, "— not for our name, or our race, or what we can do for them." He stared steadily at his brother, then, and spoke in tones that were as sharp as they were low. "If that doesn't make them our people — if that doesn't make them our *family* — I don't know what does."

The silence that followed was thick enough to feel, and heavy enough to press down on Hubert's chest as he sat there, staring across the table with a stunned expression. It lasted *forever* — at least a dozen breaths, or so — and when Hubert spoke he reached across the table with one hand and rested it on his brother's arm. "I apologize, Mason. With all my heart, I apologize. I had no idea you felt this strongly, that you had been — touched this way by these fine people. And I must apologize to Madeline, as well, I didn't know —"

Mason stirred, patted his brother's hand and interrupted him. "The proper punctuation is to put a period right there, Hubert — you didn't know. Even after two years, you thought it was just some flight of fancy by your brother — an infatuation. You didn't know — but now you do."

"Even so, I must apologize — for things said and unsaid."

Mason nodded. "Fair enough. She will be here with the children any time, now. In the meantime, though — what are you going to tell Mother? Have I lost my mind, or just my sense of perspective?" He smiled warily as he asked.

His brother shrugged. "I suppose I shall tell her the truth, little brother — that you *have* lost your perspective — and gained a new one. And, of course, that your family needs you — and you need them. Here. Where you belong."

Proper 6 / Ordinary Time 11
Mark 4:26-34

Roots

Madeline Jane Lee Randall stepped back from the serving line long enough to rewrap the scarf holding her hair back, wipe her face with her apron, and take a deep breath. She smiled down at the boy in front of her, stooped over slightly to say a quick word to him while she scooped stew onto his plate, then made a slight gesture with her head to encourage him to move on. Hubert Randall observed from his place next to her, then leaned his head closer to hers while he served potatoes onto the next boy's plate and asked, "What did you say to him?"

She laughed softly. "I reminded him that Mister Randall was going to be giving him a test on the Ten Commandments on Sunday, and he promised he would pass this one." She glanced at her brother-in-law. "Studying and memorizing are not Joey's gifts — but we expect him to try. We expect them *all* to try."

"Do they?"

She looked at him curiously. "What are you implying, Doctor Randall?"

"Hubert, if you please. I'm not implying anything, other than that you and my brother are putting an awful lot of energy into this place — these children. And to be honest, I'm not sure why."

His sister-in-law's eyes narrowed.

"I mean no disrespect," he said hastily. "No doubt you and Mason are putting forth a noble effort, for a noble people — but aren't you concerned that you're wasting your time?"

Her eyes flashed for a moment, then she sighed. "Perhaps, *Doctor* Randall, you would be so kind as to tell us *how* we're wasting our time? Is it by trying to educate them so they can fit into modern American culture — or by sharing the gospel with them, and giving them the chance to find Jesus?"

He hesitated. "You have to know that ours is a very different culture from theirs — and they are not raised in the same way, with the same values, that we are. Or were. They have their own religious beliefs, do they not?"

"Yes, of course."

"Then why do you think they — and I'm speaking about children *or* adults — would ever choose to set aside everything they've ever known, to embrace *our* culture, or our faith?"

She started to answer, stopped, and sighed again. "We're trying to give them options, Doctor. Life for them is very meager, you know — their grandfathers were promised territory where their people could live in perpetuity, however they wished — but over the years, promises have been broken, options have been stripped away. Modern society, for better or worse, surrounds them and pushes on them from every side. Many of these people will still try to cling to their ways in the face of such encroachment, but some will see the value in taking up new ways. Especially, we hope, the younger ones as they grow older."

"You hope — but how can you know? I would think you would want to *know*, if you're going to invest this kind of time." He paused. "If you're going to give up as much as you have."

"The things we've given up are things these people never had the chance to have. And that's part of it. And you're right, we can't know what the outcome is going to be, but that's no reason to not try." She looked at him from the corner of her eye as she served stew to their students. "Have you ever farmed... Hubert? Or have you ever *been* to a farm?"

"No to former, once to the latter. I went out to a farm once to treat a traumatic amputation — a thresher accident."

"Then let me put it this way: what we're doing is nothing different than any farmer does, any time he sows a field of corn. He plants the seeds, knowing not all of them are going to germinate. Knowing that not all of them will grow. Knowing that not all of them will bear fruit. He doesn't see, nor can he know, what's going on beneath the ground, as the seed starts to come to life. He never sees the roots reaching out to anchor and find nutrients. He just has faith that it will happen — but he has to do his part, first. He has to fertilize, and plant the seeds, and nurture the ones that sprout."

She looked at him directly, then, and gestured with her ladle, taking in the students who were in line or already seated at their tables, eating. "Your brother and I are in the seed planting business. We're farmers — we teach, we share the gospel, we nurture, but in the end, we never know what's going to happen… that's up to the Spirit to decide. What *is* up to us is whether or not we even try."

She paused, looking at him, then turned back to serving the last of the children in line. "Sort of like having a baby, when you think about it," she said quietly. "You carry the child, never really understanding what's going on inside of you — how it's growing, how it does what it does. All you can do is nurture it to the best of your ability and pray that your efforts come to fruition."

Hubert nodded. "That I can appreciate — there is so much that happens in places we will never see, that is just a mystery to us even as doctors — a glorious mystery, but still a mystery. We prescribe, we advise — but in the end…" He trailed off. They served in silence for a bit, then he looked up suddenly turned his head toward his sister-in-law, and raised his eyebrows.

She looked back at him and smiled, nodded slightly.

Proper 7 / Ordinary Time 12

Matthew 4:35-41

The Eye Of The Storm

Colonel Jamison Lee had just draped his tunic over the back of his folding chair and was trying to brush away the dust when he heard the tent flap rustle. He straightened up, let one hand rest casually near — but not on — the holstered Colt Navy revolver still on his hip. "Yes?"

"Captain Forrest, sir. Do you have a moment?"

"Of course," he answered, with as much enthusiasm as he could muster. It was nothing personal — just the normal let down that came at the end of such a day. A doctor friend of his had once told him that the human body contained chemicals that kept it vital and alert in times of danger, and he could believe that. When the need was there, he could be awake and active for more than a day at a stretch — but at the end of that time, those chemicals seemed to evaporate, threatening to let his body drop where he stood. Now he just wanted to do what needed to be done, and sleep.

But first, it seemed, there was a visitor to deal with.

Ian Forrest entered, still in full uniform, his tunic and pants thick with dust, stained in spots with who knew what; his boots were muddy and there was dirt on his face — a combination of earth and smudges from the black powder of whatever weapons he had been near when they fired. He smelled of sweat, fear, and death — and as Jamison studied him by the light of his kerosene lamp, he judged that the young man's expression complemented the smell.

"Have a seat, Ian. You look half-dead," he said, gesturing to the folding chair on the other side of his field desk. "What can I do for you?" he added, as Forrest sat down. The chair creaked slightly as the captain fitted his bulky frame into it; Jamison held his breath for a moment, then when it seemed the chair would hold the captain, he sat down on his own chair.

For a few moments, the two men studied one another across the desk. When it seemed obvious his visitor was struggling, Jamison spoke. "You and your boys did yourselves proud this afternoon, Ian. It was a tough day out there, but you did yourselves proud," he repeated. "You held the line."

Forrest nodded in acknowledgment, was silent for another moment or two, then sighed. "How do you do it, sir?"

Jamison leaned back, folded his arms. "Do *what*, Ian?"

"During the battle, today — in the thick of it, at the worst of it, you just sat there on your horse, calmly giving orders. When the Rebs were pushing us, and I was afraid they would breach the line, you just sat there and pointed to the gaps — told us how to plug them before they burst."

Jamison smiled. "I have a better view from horseback, Ian — it's easy to see from up there."

The young captain's head bobbed, and he went on. "It's not just that, sir — you never seemed worried. You never seemed angry. You just… told us what we needed to do, never even raised your voice more than necessary to be heard amid the battle. And your expression — it was almost *serene*. How do you do it?"

Jamison started to answer, then paused and scratched his head, leaving his hair standing up. He leaned forward. "Ian, I'll tell you the God's honest truth: I don't rightly know. I suppose if I had to put a name to it, I would say that even when the battle is hot and heavy, I can still find a quiet place in it. A quiet place in my heart. Because I feel like I'm in control — I give orders, and things get done. I try to see *everything*, and I direct my men in as rational and reasonable a way as I can. And I trust my officers — I tell you men to do something, and you *do* it." He paused, adding thoughtfully, "I don't have any illusions that nothing *can* go wrong, but I just act as though it won't — because I'm in control, and I can see what's happening, and do something to keep it from going south. There's no point in getting excited — so I don't."

"You're like Jesus," Forrest muttered, and when Jamison raised an eyebrow he said, "You know — in the boat. In the storm. On Galilee. Jesus wasn't concerned, and when they woke him up he just gave orders and it stopped. You give orders and we win, every time, and you're not even worried. Like Jesus."

Jamison nodded thoughtfully. "Okay, I get it. But let me tell you a secret — the other part of that story. And mine. The other reason Jesus was so nonchalant — and the reason I try to be, even in the thick of battle — was not just because he was in control and knew it, but because he didn't want his men to worry. He wanted *them* to know he had it under control. And so do I. So that's what I try to show them. Calm, confidence, and control."

He stood up, then, motioned for young Forrest to remain sitting. Jamison opened his trunk pulled out a bottle of bourbon and two basically clean glasses, offered one of them to his visitor. Startled, the young man just nodded. Jamison poured him a half-glass, then poured himself a half-glass as well and corked the bottle again.

He lifted the glass, inclined it toward Forrest in a toast. The captain picked up his own glass and raised it. Jamison took a sip and smiled. "But I'll tell you what, Captain. When you leave here, I want you to go find Sergeant Schwalbe, and tell him you think I'm like Jesus. I'd be interested in hearing what he says to that."

Proper 8 / Ordinary Time 13
Mark 5:21-43

Dead Girl, Live Girl

"It's creepy," Levi said, staring at the girl playing in the street. As they watched, she ran up to another girl, touched her, then ran off, laughing. The other girl immediately ran after her, then changed course to chase a smaller, slower girl, eventually cornering her by one of the other houses on the street and tagging her. With the innocent resilience of children, the game continued.

"She's my daughter," Jairus answered.

Levi barely hesitated. "It's still creepy."

"It's a *miracle*, Levi. Can't you just be happy?" There was an edge to his voice now.

"Fine. It's a creepy miracle." He looked at Jairus. "Does that make you feel better?"

"Not as much as you might think."

"Well, you better get used to it, my friend, because your precious little daughter is *always* going to be the creepy girl, and that's a fact of life, miracle or not." Levi shrugged. "It's not my doing, it's the way of the world."

"And yet *you* seem to be the one bringing it up — over and over again." Jairus gestured toward the girls playing in the street. "*They* don't seem to mind. They're just glad to have their friend back."

"In a few years, when those girls out there are settling down with husbands and having babies, that's going to change. They'll be telling their kids scary stories about what happened. And as they grow up, they're going to discover that the only things you can count on for sure in this life are dying and paying taxes." He paused. "Except for *that* girl. She changes everything. People are talking now — they'll still be talking years from now. Asking questions. Whispering behind her back. You've got to know that, Jairus."

Her father sighed and turned away, walked back into the house; Levi followed.

"It's been two days," Jairus said, "and I still can't get over the simple pleasure of just watching her play — watching her *live*." His voice dropped. "You're right, my friend — as joyous as I am, I can't forget that she was dead. And now she's not. So I have to ask: why? People die all the time. Adults die. Children die. Everybody dies. Except her. Don't get me wrong, I thank God — but I don't understand."

There was a long, heavy silence.

Finally, without looking at him, Levi said, "You're a righteous man, Jairus. You're the leader of our synagogue. Maybe the Lord chose to reward you for your righteousness."

"Am I the only righteous man in Galilee? Am I the only synagogue leader?" Jairus shook his head, let his eyes drift back toward the open door and the street beyond. "Even if that's what happened... that would mean the Lord is working through Jesus — *directly* through Jesus, just as he did through Elijah."

"I thought you were a fan."

Jairus looked at his friend. "'Fan?' I'm a follower. I've heard Jesus teach. I've heard him interpret scripture in ways I'd never thought of, but were so obvious once he finished. He's clearly a gifted teacher and interpreter and now, evidently, a prophet. But I come back to the same question: why should the Lord — or his prophet — turn his attention to me?" He sighed, shook his head again.

There was another long silence. Then Levi cleared his throat, said tentatively, "I'm no scholar, Jairus, but what if it's not about *you*?" When the synagogue leader looked at him curiously, Levi continued. "When Elijah raised the son of the widow in Zarephath, wasn't it to show that the Lord's power extended into the lands of the Gentiles — worshipers of false gods?"

"Partly," Jairus agreed.

"Then maybe the same thing is happening here?"

"That would mean we're in the position of the Gentiles, then — worshiping falsely?" Jairus paused to let that sink in. "You see how ludicrous that is, right? We worship the true God. I serve him faithfully.

I'm scrupulous about obedience to the law. I'm no idol-worshiping Gentile."

Levi shrugged. "Well — you worship the Lord as you understand you should. Maybe there's something you — we — are not getting right. Maybe there's more to it. Maybe the whole purpose is to show us that there is something beyond or more than the old way — that the old way, carried on through you, has died, but can be brought back to life by what Jesus is teaching us."

Jairus looked outside, at the bright sunlit street, and said slowly, "It's a little early in the day to be drinking, isn't it?"

Levi frowned.

"I mean, I like Jesus — I think he has a lot to teach us. But you're saying everything we know, everything we've been taught growing up, is wrong."

"Not wrong," Levi corrected. "Just — outdated, maybe. Maybe we've drifted away from how we should be living and worshiping. Maybe we've gotten too wrapped up in the what and forgotten the how and the why. The heart of it." He looked down at the floor, then at his friend. "I've been listening, too. I've heard what Jesus said."

Jairus didn't answer.

"I'm no student of scripture, like you — but if you're looking for a reason beyond just a moment of grace in your life, maybe that's it. It's what I hear, when I hear Jesus teach." Levi waited for his friend to answer, and when he didn't, he sighed. "You enjoy your daughter, Jairus — enjoy this blessing beyond all blessings. I'm sorry I offended you." He waited, again, then left in silence.

Jairus thought about calling out to him, but didn't — it seemed wrong, on some level it disturbed his heart. If there was a deeper meaning, a deeper message, could that really be it?

And then his friend was gone, leaving Jairus to sit alone, pondering the meaning of this moment of grace while he listened to the laughter of children in the street.

Proper 9 / Ordinary Time 14

Mark 6:1-13

Jesse From The Hood

Jesse Knowles sat at the table and stared at the ranks of empty chairs. As though to punctuate the complete and utter failure that had been, a single man in jeans and a gray shirt was picking them up and folding them one by one, and placing them on a rolling rack. Beyond the glass wall at the back of the room, there were plenty of people — searching card catalogs, using the free computers, browsing the shelves.

But in here, there was only Jesse, the nameless janitor — no, on second thought she could see that his name was Albert, from the patch on his shirt — and Jack, seated at Jesse's right. Jack, normally distracted by the thousand and one details of managing a campaign, was doodling on a legal pad, drawing row after row of tiny cubes, then connecting them with lines.

It was the idle setting on his brain, sort of like the old Windows screensavers that just kept repeating animated geometric shapes on the monitor. It was, he had once told her, cheaper than therapy but not as much fun as drinking.

When the silence had gone on long enough, Jesse sighed heavily and said, "I think we can safely say that this was a disaster." She looked at Jack. "I'm afraid the only logical step, at this point, is for me to fire you."

"Last week in Springfield," he said, still doodling, "you fired me for not renting a large enough hall for your rally, which meant that there were people outside who never got to see you. Two weeks before that, you fired me for not getting you an interview with that YouTube influencer — that former Miss Whatever-She-Was who's now a lifestyle coach. I don't know which word I hate more, 'influencer' or 'lifestyle coach.'" He lifted pen from paper and looked up at her. "If you keep firing me, I'm going to start taking this personally."

"Let me know if that happens, and I'll think about easing up." She leaned back in her chair, lifting the front legs off the floor. The janitor noticed and shot her a look; she put the legs back on the floor and waved a hand to him. "Sorry, Albert." He went back to folding chairs. She shook her head, tilted it back and forth to each side to stretch her neck muscles. "I don't get it. How could this happen, this late in the campaign?"

"It's not that big a deal. You're tired. This is good, you can turn in early tonight, and be rested for your rally tomorrow in Bay City. That reminds me, you have to get up early — it's a five hour drive. We want to be there beforehand, so you can be ready to knock 'em dead."

"I know. But *can* I be ready?" She gestured toward the empty chairs. "I drew, like, three people to this town hall — and two of them were reporters."

"Don't forget the homeless guy who was looking for the bathroom."

"Fine, four people. At least *he* had an intelligent question. But how can I draw nobody to a town hall in my own hometown? I grew up here, Jack. I went to school here and I worked my first couple of jobs here. How can there be this *little* interest in my campaign in my own hometown?"

Jack sniffed and sighed. "Human nature, Jesse. First of all — be honest — you haven't lived here since you went to college."

"But I still grew up here."

"And I think that's maybe why you didn't have more people."

"What do you mean?"

"I mean it's a small town. You look back, and you think, yeah, this is where I started. This was my launch pad. People here — they don't think of you as a politician. They never even really saw you as an adult. To them, you're still the kid who made walrus tusks with French fries, and stuck beans in her nose to make other kids laugh."

Her eyebrows drew together. "I never did either of those things."

"Really? I thought everyone did, as a kid."

"No, everyone didn't. Did you?"

"We're not talking about me. We're talking about you, and about how if your homies ever think of you at all, they're probably thinking about you as you were way back when — as a kid."

"Homies? Am I Jesse from the hood, now?"

Jack shrugged.

"This town doesn't *have* a hood, Jack. You've seen it."

"The principle's the same."

"And it wasn't *way* back. But it's been awhile," she added truthfully.

"It's nothing personal — it's not like they hate you. *That* would have gotten people to turn out. It's just, to them, you're still that kid. Just like every other kid. And they're not going to think of you any differently, right now." He shrugged again. "That's just how it is. You didn't make a name for yourself while you were here, so you're stuck on what you were when you left. A kid."

"Great. It's like being perpetually at the kids' table at Thanksgiving."

"Right. Until you *do* make a name here. If you win the primary, and go on to the general, maybe you'll be able to do something for them, here, that will make a name for yourself. But until then…" He trailed off.

She nodded. "I get it. Until then, it's on to the next town."

"Exactly." He stood up. "So let's go — we've got votes to find and problems to solve."

Proper 10 / Ordinary Time 15

Mark 6:14-29

The Deal

Jesse Knowles looked at the paper in her hand, flipped the page and folded it back, then flipped to the third and last page, studied it and set it down on her desk. "Okay, Holt, what was I looking at?"

"I've been doing some work, Ms. Knowles — quite a bit of work, actually," the man in the chair opposite her said. He leaned forward and tapped the paper with his finger. "What you have here is a list of commitments — very valuable commitments. I have secured a commitment to donate to your campaign from every donor on that list, in the amount next to their name."

Jesse reached for the paper again, started to scan it.

"I'll save you some mental math, Ms. Knowles — that's two hundred and thirty thousand dollars you have in your hand. With the election just a month away, in a four point race, I thought it might come in handy."

She nodded thoughtfully, studying the names; some of them were people her campaign had been pursuing for months. "Holt," she said slowly, "you have no idea how much we need this injection of cash." She raised her eyes from the page, looked at her visitor and smiled. "I thank you — the party thanks you. When can we expect the checks to come in?"

Holt sat back in his chair, clasped his hands over his stomach. "Any day, now, Ms. Knowles, any day. There is one thing, though — after speaking to the people on that list, there was one thing they almost all had in common. One thing that… let's say needs to be remedied, before they can feel good about donating their money."

Jesse's smile changed, becoming a frozen expression. "Ah. I'm sensing tension, here."

"No, no, no," Holt said quickly, "Nothing so… quid pro quo. It's not a string, Ms. Knowles. But these are pragmatic people, with an understanding of the political arena. What they need is some acknowledgment of a problem they see with your campaign. A problem they feel needs to be resolved quickly, before it derails any chance you have at getting elected."

The smile faded, now. "And that problem is?"

Holt leaned forward, locked eyes with her and moved forward slightly in his seat. "Jack. Your campaign manager. He needs to go."

She raised her eyebrows. "Jack? He's the best there is, Holt, and he's my friend. I've got no problem saying — saying to any of *them* — that he's the reason I've made it this far. Why do they think he's a problem?"

Holt hesitated, drumming his fingers on his leg, then shrugged and said, "It's this simple, Ms. Knowles. He rubs me the wrong way."

The candidate gave a short, barking laugh. "He rubs *everyone* the wrong way, Holt — that's kind of what he does. He knows more about politics than any two people I've ever met, but he's not a politician. Hell, he prides himself on that."

"Ms. Knowles, you're aiming for the big leagues now — and Jack Hagen is not a big league player. In your heart, I think you know that — and right there, on your desk, is almost a quarter of a million dollars in pledges from some very smart, very tuned-in people who know it, too. I want to help you, and they want to help you, too — but there's helping, and then there's just throwing your money away. Nobody wants to do that. I'm sure you can appreciate that."

Jesse looked down at the list, touched it with her fingers, studied the names.

"Ms. Knowles, the word on the street is that your campaign just canceled a two hundred thousand dollars ad buy, scheduled for the weekend before the election. There's also talk that you may be letting some of your paid staff go — and we all know that this is the exact wrong time to be doing that. Right there, is the solution to your problems. And the key to your future. You're a smart woman, and a good politician — you can do a lot for your constituents, if you get in. But second place never accomplished a darn thing."

Jesse frowned. "No... I don't suppose it ever did."

Holt smiled, then, and leaned back in his chair. "Right. Just do this one thing, and you can win — we *all* can win. It's the logical thing to do."

She nodded slowly. "I suppose it is."

#

Jack Hagen entered her office without knocking, dropped down in the chair opposite her. "You called? Where were you — I tried to reach you a couple of hours ago and went right to voicemail."

"Sorry, did you leave a message?"

He made a short raspberry sound, dismissed the idea with a wave of his hand. "I hate those things. Nobody ever calls you back, anyway."

"Maybe because you never leave a message."

"Chicken, egg — who can say? You called?"

"I was in a meeting, with Holt Steinberg."

"During daylight? He usually only comes out at night."

"This is serious." She took out the list, held it in her hand.

"Sorry. I'll put on my serious face." He blinked, stared at her impassively.

"Right. So here's the deal: last night you told me what kind of shape we were in as far as money. This morning — during daylight — Holt brought me this list of 'donors' who were willing to commit to almost a quarter of a million dollars." She put the list down on the desk, slid it across. "With one stipulation."

"A pound of flesh? Maybe a newborn baby, with some fava beans and a nice chianti?"

"Just you. Gone. Today."

There was a short silence, then, "Oh. I see. Well, he's never forgiven me for swapping out the dirt in his coffin for kitty litter."

"I'm serious. He's serious. He can give us two hundred and thirty thousand dollars — enough to get us out of this jam — in exchange for me dropping you from the campaign."

"Right." He stood up. "Do you want my resignation, or does the deal include duckwalking me out of here with a police escort?"

"Sit down. What I want is for you to start calling these people and telling them their generosity is being used to blackmail our campaign — and ask if they were aware of it. And it might not hurt to mention that there's a written list floating around out there, and you're hoping to be able to track it down and quash it."

He sat down, picked up the list and glanced at it. "Wow. Remind me never to make *you* mad." He looked at her, then. "But these are some pretty high-powered folks, Jesse. And these are some big numbers. Are you sure you wouldn't rather just take the deal? It could mean the difference between winning and losing."

The candidate shook her head. "I don't care. There are deals that are worth it and deals that aren't — and deals that take a little piece of your soul with them. I won't do it. I'm no King Herod, Holt Steinberg is no Salome — and I'm not serving your head up on a platter to *anyone*."

For the slightest of moments, her campaign manager just stared at her, silently.

She let the moment pass, then waved toward the door. "Don't you have calls to make?"

Proper 11 / Ordinary Time 16

Mark 6:30-34,53-56

Marathon Men

"Jee-*sus*!"

"Jee-*sus*!"

"Jee-*sus*!"

A couple of the disciples were lowering the sail, so the commandeered fishing boat was barely gliding through the water when the noise of the crowd reached them. A knot of people had gathered on the shore, chanting as more streamed from north and south to join them. "How do they do it?" Thomas wondered out loud, eyes slit as he stared at the crowd. "We should be moving faster than they can walk — how do they follow us? How do they know?"

It was not a real question, but Matthew answered it, though his voice was also low. "Five hundred years ago, the Persians sent an army up against the Athenians. The Greeks met them on the beach at a place called Marathon, and after they drove the Persians into the sea a Greek soldier named Pheidippides ran the entire way from Marathon to Athens — 26 miles, like running from one end of the Sea of Galilee to the other and back again — just to tell the Athenians that they'd won."

"So you're telling me these people are Greek?"

"Not on the Galilean side of the sea. I'm just telling you it can be done."

"So you're telling me these people are like, what, this Marathon guy — Pheidippi-what?"

"Pheidippides. And no. He was a trained soldier, a courier. I'm just saying people are capable of covering a substantial distance fairly quickly, with the right incentive."

"And the incentive is what? To make sure we never eat another meal in peace? To make sure the Master never has another moment of quiet? I want to know — because ever since we got back, it has been like nonstop craziness. Even the Master's had enough of it — that's why we

Proper 11 / Ordinary Time 16

borrowed this boat and tried to find a quiet place to eat lunch and talk to one another without a thousand ears listening in." He waved a hand toward the shore. "And then *this* happens. Like someone figured out where we were going, and somehow let the whole world know."

"Thomas... Matthew... it's hardly the whole world," a voice said gently, behind them. Thomas closed his eyes, hung his head for a moment, then raised it and turned to look at the source of the voice. Jesus smiled back at him, nodded toward the shoreline, drawing ever closer. "There can't be more than a couple hundred people there. It's not the whole world — it's not even an appreciable fraction of Galilee."

"But why? A hundred or a thousand, why can't they leave us alone — just for a little while?" Thomas asked. "You have to be exhausted — we are, just trying to manage the crowd."

"These are *our* people, Thomas — the ones I was sent here to save. The fact that they follow us — that just confirms we're reaching the right people." He raised a hand to shade his eyes, studied the growing knot of people, listened to the chants. "Have you ever been sick, Thomas? I mean *really* sick. Coughing, fever, all the rest?"

Thomas shook his head. "No, Rabbi."

"Do you know anyone who was?"

He shrugged. "Sure."

"What did they do?"

"Mostly home remedies, I guess. I had an uncle who actually went to a physician. He could afford it."

Another shrug. "He died. Most of them did."

"Exactly. And people know that. If they get seriously ill — I mean *seriously* ill — or become blind, or paralyzed, or deaf... there is nothing anyone can do. Historically, there's never been anything *anyone* could do." Jesus paused, smiled again. "Until now. Until me. Just the same as no one is able to enter into the kingdom of heaven on their own. Is it really any wonder that they follow me?"

"But I thought you weren't all about the miracles? You've said that before."

"And I'm not — I'm here to teach, to heal the brokenness of a sinful world, to bring the kingdom of heaven to people... and to show love for my Father's children. So if that means I heal them of their physical infirmities, then so be it."

"But you can't heal everyone, Master," Thomas said.

"Perhaps, perhaps. But let me ask you this: if you were walking by the side of the sea and saw ten men drowning, would you try to save the ones you could — or would you throw up your hands and say, 'since I can't save everyone, I won't worry about saving *anyone*?'"

"Well, no, of course not —"

"Or if you were talking to friends, eating your dinner — would you say you don't want to be disturbed, and let them drown?"

"I'm not a monster."

"Neither am I. You're right, I have tried to find peace, sometimes, but if these people still find me… if there is still something I can do for someone who is right there in my presence… I'm going to do it." He put his hand on Thomas' shoulder, then, and added, "I guess the question, then, is: are you willing to help me?"

Thomas looked to shore, now almost close enough that they could ground their boat and walk to it; there were people as far as his eyes could see from his seat on the boat. Young and old, some lying on mats, some with bandaged eyes and someone else leading them — others just excited, anxious to hear from this Galilean prophet.

It would be a thousand years before playing cards would be invented — but Thomas still knew when they were stacked against him. He shook his head and shrugged. "What else can I do, Rabbi? Tell me how to help, and I will."

Jesus smiled. "That's all I ask, Thomas. That's all I ever ask of you."

Proper 12 / Ordinary Time 17

John 6:1-21

Anything He Can Do…

The bustle of activity that was the temple during the day was starting to fade away. The sun was dipping below the hills to the west, and the offering of sacrifices had ceased for the day, though the fire of the altar still burned brightly and the scent of sacrifice — a mixture of incense and death — still rose on pillars of smoke toward the heavens, there to be smelled and appreciated, so it was said, by God.

Isaiah, a temple scribe, took Judas by the arm and walked him away from the altar, past the tables of slaughter toward a corner of the priest's court; sometimes even the Lord's business was best conducted away from the prying eyes of the idly curious. When they were out of earshot, as well, Isaiah stopped and looked at Judas, shook his head reproachfully.

"What?" the disciple asked defensively.

"Your boy seems to have set himself an ambitious goal," the scribe answered.

"What do you mean?"

"I was reflecting on your reports —"

"I don't report to you, scribe. Don't make this something it's not." Reflexively, Judas looked around to see if anyone was paying attention; they were not.

"Sorry — I was reflecting on our conversations," the scribe amended graciously — though with a hint of sarcasm. "And I realized, during prayer this morning, that your Galilean friend is not just trying to assume the mantle of a prophet, but is trying to outdo one of our most revered prophets. He's trying to show himself to be better, more powerful than the great Elisha, himself."

The disciple shook his head doubtfully. "I don't understand."

"Read the scriptures, my friend, read the scriptures. Elisha miraculously caused a woman to not run out of oil — your rabbi appeared to miraculously change ordinary water into wine. Elisha's supplications brought the Shunammite child back to life — the Galilean has restored two to life, by your own words. And the bread, of course: Elisha caused twenty loaves of bread to feed a hundred men — one loaf for every five men. Jesus used five loaves to feed five thousand — a loaf for every *thousand* men." The scribe shook his head again. "The Greeks have a word — *hubris*. Your boy has it."

"Does he, though? Jesus makes no secret of the fact that these miracles come from the Lord; he just prays for them. The same as the healings that flow through him." Judas shook his head. "I see many faults in the man, but hubris is not one."

"Don't be deceived, Judas, a man can reek of self-promotion and self-service even while he is pretending to be humble. No one else can do the things he does, can they?"

Judas shrugged. "He sent us out, once, on our own, and some were able to heal, or cast out demons."

Isaiah looked at him sharply. "You never mentioned this. Did you engage in this fraud, as well?"

"No, no, nothing of the sort — though I tried. I prayed, the same as him, but nothing came of it. That's part of what brought me to you."

"So if you need more evidence that the man is either a straight-up fraud or in league with false gods, you have it right there, don't you?"

"But you say he's trying to set himself up as better and more powerful than Elisha — and I tell you I have never seen that in anything he's done. In three years, I have never once heard Jesus say that he is more powerful, or stronger, than *any* prophet. If anything, he does the exact opposite of brag."

"And again I tell you, a great show of meekness and humility can be just as powerful a way of proclaiming your greatness as actually claiming it. This man you follow claims no formal study of scripture, and yet he is able to relate himself to passages from the prophets, well-known and obscure. And now, I realize how he is tapping into stories of old that many of the faithful may only half-remember and using those to his own advantage." He touched Judas' arm, looked at him sincerely. "Surely you can see that, my friend, can't you?"

Proper 12 / Ordinary Time 17

"But — the five thousand. I was there. There was this massive crowd, Isaiah, and they needed to be fed. Even if we had somehow gone to every village around us and taken every loaf of bread we could find, there would not have been enough to feed them all. And yet, Jesus made it happen. He prayed, and it happened. No peals of thunder, no mighty winds — just people eating, getting their fill. If there was ever a greater reminder of God's generosity, or of how God provided food for our ancestors even in the wilderness, I don't know what it would be."

"And there's the danger," Isaiah said simply. "Jesus uses the situation to recall God's miracle of manna — recapitulating it, even if he doesn't come right out and say so — and then he becomes the vehicle for how it occurs here and now. He sets himself up as Moses, for all practical purposes. Surely you can see how dangerous that is."

"But then when he heard rumors that some were planning to force him to be their king, he left. Quickly."

Isaiah sighed. "Have you ever seen a woman flirt with a man by turning down his advances? The more she does so, the more the man convinces himself that he must have her. I fear it's the same with your teacher."

There was a long silence. "I don't want to believe you," Judas said finally.

"But you do, don't you?" Isaiah answered.

"How can I know for sure what his intent is?" Judas asked softly. "I need to know."

"And so do we. Just keep following him — and watching. Watch for the so-called miracles and see how they feed into his quest for power and adoration. And then come back and tell me about it." He put his arm around Judas' shoulder, and began walking him toward the gate. "I'll be happy to help you see the truth. It's what I'm here for."

They were walking past the altar when Judas stopped suddenly, seemed to think for a moment — then turned to the scribe. "About the five thousand..." he began.

Proper 13 / Ordinary Time 18
John 6:24-35

The Bread Of Life

If the crowd had been better organized, they might have been called a delegation. As it was, they were just a handful of the loudest voices in the crowd, self-elected to call upon the prophet from Nazareth. They found him outside of Capernaum, sitting with his disciples in what was the quietest time they'd had in days... maybe weeks.

They stopped at the outer circle of followers and shouted to Jesus, "Where were you? How did you get here?"

The man from Nazareth just smiled mysteriously, well aware that they would not believe an honest answer. He turned his attention back to his companions, spoke to them in soft tones that were not quite audible to those standing on the fringe of the cluster around him. Frustrated, they spoke over him. "When did you get here? Where did you come from? We were searching for you."

"What, is it breakfast time already?" Peter shot back ironically, and laughed; the others joined in, except for Jesus. Jesus raised one finger, wagged it from side to side as though to say *no, that's not what we do*.

Speaking to the representatives of the crowd, then, he said, "Is that it, are you seeking more food?" They did not answer, but looked on expectantly, and he sighed. "You're here because you ate your fill of bread last night, and now you're hungry again. You think the sign that I brought to you is that you were all able to eat, and you hope to see another sign and wonder today. Yes?"

There were a few nods, then, a couple of grumbled of agreement.

Jesus stood up, stepped toward them. "Friends, you are looking for the wrong miracle. You're looking for the bread of this world — the bread that filled your bellies yesterday — but the bread you *should* be seeking is the bread of heaven. You should pray for the bread that comes from God and never runs out or grows stale."

"Where is this bread?" the self-appointed delegates demanded. "Tell

Proper 13 / Ordinary Time 18

us where we can find it and eat our fill."

Jesus stood up. "You have found it. Your forefathers had manna in the wilderness, to sustain them when there was nothing else. You have me. I am the bread of life — the very bread of heaven, sent to you by God so that you might have life, and not darkness."

"Are you greater than Moses, then?" another in the group demanded, unconsciously glancing at the sky as though ready to dodge any lightning bolts that might find their way.

"Moses could not — cannot — give you the true bread of heaven. God alone can do that, and God has done it, through me."

They fell back, then, pulling away from Jesus and his disciples to argue among themselves over what he had said; Jesus watched them with an amused expression. The disciples were silent — except for Judas, who leaned close to Jesus and said, "You must be careful, Rabbi. These people do not understand — they may think that you are declaring yourself to be God himself." Judas paused there, shot him a look that said, *but you're not, are you?*

"They can think whatever they wish," Jesus said quietly. "The truth is: I am God's son, and God sent me here to bring life to our people. Just as bread sustains the body, the bread of heaven — the spiritual sustenance that comes from God — sustains the spirit, and it is the spirit with which I concern myself." He looked at Judas curiously. "Do you still not understand? I am the sustenance for any and all who wish to live in the kingdom of heaven."

Judas looked doubtful.

Jesus looked up at the sky, then back to his followers. "Think of a plant. Give it fertilizer and water, but deprive it of the light which the Lord gives us from the sun, and it will perish. The simple physical sustenance of this world isn't enough for a plant, or for a person. Without the light of the sun, or the light that comes from God, they will be stunted forever."

"So the bread, yesterday — all the bread. It was your way — God's way — of saying that by following you, those people would never go hungry," Thomas said, thinking it through as he said it.

Jesus nodded. "Spiritually, yes — if they put their trust in me, they will never hunger for spiritually sustenance again."

He was about to say more when the others returned — so he just smiled and looked at them expectantly, waiting to explain it all again.

Proper 14 / Ordinary Time 19

John 6:35, 41-51

Who Do You Think You Are?

The "delegation" from the crowd, bolstered by the addition of a few others, returned and stood a short distance away from Jesus. One of them — Jesus thought he recognized the face — stepped past his companions and said angrily, "Who do you think you are, Jesus? You come to us claiming to have come down from heaven, but *I* know you're the son of Joseph bar Heli and his wife, Mary. You used to sit in the mud in Nazareth and make bread from dirt."

Jesus looked at the man, raised an eyebrow and waited.

When he realized what he'd said, the man blustered, "Not *real* bread — just dirt made into loaves. You know what I mean," he finished lamely, as the disciples chuckled, and his companions looked down at their feet.

A woman spoke next. "I remember your parents, Jesus. Your mother found herself with child *very* soon after they married, didn't she?"

"I could hardly know that, could I?" he asked reasonably, refusing to take the bait.

He paused then, silently took a few moments to look each of them in the face individually, taking his time even as the silence stretched to an uncomfortable length. When he spoke, he said quietly, "I come here to tell you who I *am* — not who I *was*. Moses was a foundling, then a prince of Egypt, then a murderer — and finally a prophet who led our ancestors out of Egypt. David was born a shepherd, became a warrior, and went on to be the greatest king in our history. How or to whom I was born does not mean nearly as much as why I was born and what I am here to do."

Jesus stood up and raised his arms, as though seeking to embrace the entire world. "Brothers and sisters, I was born to bring light to the world, to banish the darkness of human sin. And I was born to be the bread of life to this world. To you."

He stepped toward them, now, arms still open. "Bread made with the grains of the earth may stop the rumbling in your belly, for a time — it may satisfy the cravings of the body, but eventually you will be hungry again. But I come to you with something new: the bread that I offer — the bread that I *am* — will satisfy the hunger, fill the empty place in your heart and soul forever. I am life, the very essence of creation sent to dwell among you — eat of my flesh, and you will be renewed forever."

There was a murmur from the crowd. "Eat your flesh? Are we barbarians, now?"

Judas, who was standing behind Jesus, looked down, shook his head and muttered under his breath, "He's gone too far. Too far." Thomas looked at him questioningly, but he just shook his head again. "Our Master has lost his mind."

"Give him a chance," Thomas answered, looking back at Jesus. "He speaks of very difficult things."

"Difficult because they are mad."

Thomas shushed him, leaned toward Jesus.

"John the Baptizer called me the Lamb of God, so remember this: the flesh of the lamb is consumed at Passover, and it is a holy remembrance of our flight from Egypt. On that night, too, the blood of the lamb was spilled, to signify to the angel of death that faithful Jews lived there." Jesus answered. "So, too, must I be consumed if you are to be freed from the bondage of darkness; so must my blood be shed. I tell you now, that my body will be consumed by the darkness of this world to fulfill what is written, but even then light *will* prevail. This body will return to you so that you might know God's grace and forgiveness. Only by freely consuming the life that is me, will you find life in the kingdom of heaven."

The voices from the crowd were louder and angrier, and one voice came through loudly and clearly: "Jesus of Nazareth, if you are who you say you are, show us another sign. Perform another wonder, that we might believe you come from heaven."

Jesus looked heavenward for a moment, then back to his own disciples — and then to the crowd starting to press in around them. When he spoke, his voice cut through the noise of the crowd. "God does not perform wonders to change the hearts and minds of men, but to open them," he answered, lowering his arms. "I am who I am. The truth is not a show to be put on for the weak of faith. The bread of my flesh is enough."

As he finished speaking, he turned away and withdrew from the crowd. His disciples hesitated, then followed after — except for Judas, who stared after him with a mix of frustration and sadness. The crowd stood still as well, as though the effort to understand robbed them of the ability to move.

"Ah, Jesus — Rabbi — what have you done?" Judas sighed, and pondered what he should do next.

Proper 15 / Ordinary Time 20
John 6:51-58

The Way To Life

Jamison Lee was sitting at his desk — a folding camp desk that had somehow been erroneously reported as destroyed in battle when he was mustering out at the end of the war between the states — when he realized he was not alone. Knowing that Libby and their daughter were in Milwaukee, visiting her grandmother, the choices of who it might be were limited. Without looking up from the sermon he was writing — well, *trying* to write — he said, "Two Bucks, my friend — what brings you here on a Saturday night?" Then he did look up and smiled at his oldest friend on the reservation.

His friend did not smile in return, which was typical. "Reverend Lee, I hope I am not disturbing you, but I have been troubled all week by your gospel-book lesson last Sunday."

"You're not the first to struggle with it, my friend, and you won't be the last. Come, have a seat."

His visitor sat on a wooden folding chair and looked at him nervously. "I want to be a good Christian, reverend, but this gospel-book lesson where Jesus tells his followers that they must eat his flesh and drink his blood to live gives me trouble. I am a simple man, living the simple ways of my people, and those ways have *never* said we must eat the flesh and blood of another person. There are stories old women tell young children, about creatures who used to be men, who live in the woods and eat flesh — but those are just stories, meant to remind children that there can be danger in the forest."

Jamison nodded. "Right — scary stories, not stories meant to tell us how to live."

"Yes, reverend. And yet, Jesus tells his tribe this is what they *must* do."

"It is a puzzle, isn't it? I remember, a long time ago when I was just in my teens, reading in the newspaper about a wagon train heading out to California. They left Illinois later in the year than they should have, and to try to make up time they took what they thought was a shortcut through the mountains. They ended up being trapped by deep snow and spent the winter there without enough food to survive."

"So they died?" Two Bucks asked.

Jamison shook his head ruefully. "Not all of them. Some lived — about half, I think — and when the rescuers found the bodies of those who didn't, they discovered that some of them had been eaten. None of the survivors would talk about it, but only insisted that nobody had been murdered. These people — they were called the Donner Party, if I remember — they've lived out their lives under a cloud of disgust and suspicion."

"So were they Christian?" Two Bucks asked, his expression intent as he tried to follow what Jamison was saying.

"No, no — well, maybe. But that's not the point I'm trying to make. The point is, they were reviled —" He hesitated. "They were looked down upon with disgust by the whole nation, for what they were suspected of doing. Eating of flesh, what we call cannibalism, is almost universally considered to be a sin of the highest kind — what we call taboo. Something you just don't do under any circumstances."

"And was it the same in the time of Jesus, when the gospel-book was written?"

"It was the same. People have struggled with this teaching for two thousand years, more or less."

"If it is so difficult, why did Jesus teach it? If it is a good thing, as a thing from God should be, why is it so hard to accept?"

Jamison chuckled and leaned across the space between them, patted his friend on the shoulder. "Two Bucks, you sound like my professor in seminary. I will tell you what he told us. He said that at its heart, what Jesus was saying is that he, himself, is the light of the world, and the source of life, and if someone — a sinner, like any of us — wants to live, we must turn to him as the source of life. We must take in and make a part of us all that he teaches. We must make the very essence of how he lived a part of us. We must, if we want to inherit the kingdom of heaven, leave our darkness behind and instead take in the light that he brings to the world."

Two Bucks nodded, his brow furrowed. "If we want to build our own muscles, we must consume the muscles of other creatures, is that it?"

"That's a really good analogy — way to look at it. I think you have it. To become what we admire, or aspire to be, we must make it a part of us. Jesus just used some very shocking language, in which the image of his physical being was used to represent who he was spiritually. Professor Schunemann said that because this was a new idea, Jesus used that shocking language to kind of wake people up and make them really think about what he was saying."

Two Bucks leaned back in his chair, ignoring the creaking of it, and shook his head. "Why must his teachings be so hard? If Jesus wanted people to believe and follow him, why did he make it so difficult to understand?"

"Well — my professor would tell you that Jesus knew imagery, even shocking imagery — was easier to remember than just words. But more importantly, I think Jesus wanted his people to really think about what he was saying. Discussion and discernment, not blind obedience, because discussion and discernment come from the heart, and it's easier to hold onto your beliefs if you've struggled to get them than if you just accept the words of others."

Two Bucks seemed to be turning this idea over in his mind for a bit, then he nodded and stood up. "Thank you, Reverend Lee. I think I can sleep tonight."

Jamison stood up as well. "You're welcome, Two Bucks. Unfortunately, I cannot — not until I get this done for tomorrow." He waited until his friend left, then sat down behind his desk again and stared at the blank paper.

Why is it so hard, indeed? he wondered.

Proper 16 / Ordinary Time 21

John 6:56-69

Tapping Out

"What do you need?" Jesse Knowles asked, "I'm kind of busy."

"That's okay," Jack Hagen answered, "this won't take long."

Before she could respond, he used his arm to push aside paper and knickknacks on her desk to clear a space for the legal pad he dropped on it, then pulled over a chair and sat down. "Here's the thing," he said, leaning over the desk and beginning to sketch. "Last year, there were 64,000 babies born in this state."

He drew a horizontal line across the pad with a slash of his marker, freehanded a bell curve, then divided it with a couple of dashed vertical lines, one toward each end of the curve. "Using the arbitrary but reasonable 10-80-10 rule, we can say that about 51,000 of these babies were average-looking —" He scrawled that number in the middle of the curve. "— leaving us with about 6,500 babies who were exceptionally good looking —" he wrote that number over the far right end of the curve, "— and about 6,500 ugly ones." He wrote that number over the left end of the curve, put an exclamation point at the end of it, tapped it with his finger and looked at her.

"Now, Candidate Knowles — can you tell me why in the name of all that is holy, you would tell 6,500 mothers that their children are ugly? Or, better yet, *13,000* parents, nearly all of whom are voting age?"

"Now, Jack, I never did any such thing. There's no such thing as an ugly baby, and you know it."

"*That* is a canard, foisted upon the public by big baby. We can all name at least one ugly baby — my niece's youngest is a good example; I'd show you a picture, but I don't carry one anymore. But our social norm is that you don't say it. Ever. *Just like you don't ever say that part of the problem with public schools today is the students.* You told umpteen thousand parents — God knows it's *way* more than thirteen thousand — that their kids are dumb. Or delinquents. Or both. Did you decide you really don't want to get elected? Or were you tired of being tied for first in the polls?"

"All I did was answer a question. Honestly. In case you haven't noticed in the last year and a half, it's what I do."

"Yes, and it's refreshing, right up to the point where it becomes a self-inflicted wound. We've talked about this, haven't we? There is a time for discretion — usually it's when some joker with a microphone and an axe to grind catches you in public and tries to pin you down on something complex and controversial. There's no shame in telling the person to read your position paper and then come to you with questions if he has any."

"We don't *have* a position paper on why test scores have leveled off, or even dropped, in the last ten years."

"Then that would be an excellent assignment for your staff. Your answer, then, is to say it's a complex issue that you've been studying for a while, and you'll be issuing a paper in the very near future. Because it *is* a complex issue, and you can't reasonably be expected to come up with a solution off the top of your head."

"I'm not sure it's that complex. Kids are starting kindergarten less ready than they ever have. Between TV and the internet, their brains are being turned into sponges that can retain useless pop culture trivia but can't tell you who was president during the Civil War. Teachers are forced to deal with children who are clearly not ready for school, or capable of attending to what's going on in the classroom, and while they're doing that they're losing valuable teaching time when they *could* be educating the kids who are actually ready to learn. And if you dare to say anything to the parents, *you're* the one with a problem, because their precious little baby couldn't possibly be at fault."

Halfway through, her campaign manager laid his head on her desk and gently bumped it with his forehead as though keeping time. When she finished, he raised his head, sat up again in his chair, and said, "*Or*, you could say there are many aspects to that question, and when you're in office you plan to explore solutions like attracting better teachers and decreasing class sizes, or other options."

"By and large, I don't believe the teachers are the problem. Better principals I could get behind —"

"Good, tick off school administrators, too."

"But my point is, I understand the real problems. If education is going to be a central issue, then I'm going to tell the truth as I've seen it to be."

"And you're going to lose."

"Then at least I'll lose honestly." She stared at his sketch for a few moments. "How bad is it?"

"We've lost a few donors — and some volunteers. Like, sixty or seventy."

"Right. That's not good. But —"

"You're being honest, I know." He ran a hand through his hair, wiped his forehead and said, "Look, Jesse, this is how it is: a lot of people, they come work for a campaign or a candidate because it looks like it might be fun, and it gives them a chance to feel like they're part of something special. And then when it stops being fun, they leave. They don't have a real investment, or a real understanding of who the candidate is, and what it takes to win."

"Okay, I can see that."

"But if you're lucky — and by lucky I mean if you're honest, and you tell it to them straight — your core people are going to stick it out. Because we do understand who you are, and we do know you're telling the truth. And we still believe."

"So are you telling me I still have a chance?"

Jack grunted. "That is a whole different question, Ms. Knowles — I'll have a better answer for you tomorrow, after I've had a chance to bend some ears. So if it's all the same to you, I'll be gone now — and I'd appreciate it if you could keep a low profile for the day."

Jesse Knowles smiled. "I will. After I talk to the guy from CNN who's meeting me in twenty minutes." She shrugged. "I promised him yesterday."

"I know — you keep your promises."

Proper 17 / Ordinary Time 22

Mark 7:1-8, 14-15, 21-23

Garbage In, Garbage Out?

Some people have the gift of directness — they are able to sit down to a difficult conversation and dive right into it. Others take a more nuanced approach, creeping up on the topic in a sideways fashion that allows participants to suddenly realize they're in the midst of the discussion without warning.

And then there are those who never quite seem to get there without prompting.

Belinda Posey was one of the latter.

Fifteen minutes into the conversation, Margaret Randall was still not sure what it was about. The chair of the Ladies' Auxiliary had spoken about the weather, the upcoming silent auction, school, and her sneaking suspicion that the Beatles' *Abbey Road* album had been recorded under the influence of mind altering substances. When she circled back to school, Margaret took the plunge and decided that Mrs. Posey was there to talk about something happening at school.

With a subtle — but not *too* subtle — look at her watch, Margaret said, "Mrs. Posey, I'm going to be meeting my husband for lunch in about fifteen minutes. Is there something going on at school that I should know about?"

"Well —" she answered uncertainly, "— it's about Mr. Borden, he's the ninth grade English teacher at Wilson Junior High."

Margaret nodded. "Yes, my daughter had him for home room last year."

"My son is in his third hour English class, and he told me something very... disturbing. I wanted to talk to you, teacher to teacher, and ask if you could maybe bring it up with the pastor." She looked embarrassed. "I don't want to — I don't think it's my place."

And yet, it's your place to make a complaint, Margaret thought to herself, and smiled. "Well, I'm quite sure John would be opening to listening to you, but if there's something you want me to bring to him, I'd be happy to do that."

"Wonderful." Mrs. Posey sat for a moment, gathering either her thoughts or her courage, and then said, "I'm afraid there's something very, very wrong about Mr. Borden. He's done something totally inappropriate, and somebody needs to say something to him. I'm not even sure if he shouldn't be fired."

"What did he do, Mrs. Posey?" Margaret pressed.

"About two weeks ago, with the end of the quarter coming up, he gave the class an extra credit assignment. He said that anyone who went to see *Easy Rider* at the theater and then wrote an essay about what it said to them about life in America today could get up to a hundred points." She paused for dramatic effect. "Mrs. Randall, *Easy Rider* is an R-rated film."

"I'm aware, Mrs. Posey," she said, without adding that she knew because she and her husband had driven to Green Bay to see it right after it was released.

"Isn't it *awful*, Mrs. Randall!? I mean, encouraging our children to flaunt the law that way is… it's downright anarchistic."

"Well — movie ratings don't have the force of law, Mrs. Posey. Giving a film an R or an X rating doesn't mean minors are legally forbidden from seeing it. That's up to the theaters — and the parents — to enforce. But on the other hand, I do agree that encouraging students to flout the rules is probably not the best choice he could have made." She hesitated. "On still another hand, critics are calling it an important film, and it does have a lot to say about modern society, so I can see why he might think it was important for them to see it."

"But shouldn't that be their parents' choice?"

"Of course — but the fact that it was extra credit, and not a regular assignment, makes it look like he was leaving room for the kids to have that discussion with their parents."

"Surely you're not defending him?"

"No, not at all. But I'm saying there's room for discussion here."

"But I heard there were a lot of drugs, and bad language, and —" she lowered her voice, "— sex. Kids shouldn't be seeing those things. Life is hard enough, without movies corrupting them."

Margaret smiled. "I think our kids are a little more resilient than that. I'm a lot more concerned with what they *do* than what they *see*."

Mrs. Posey looked at her closely. "You seem to be very blasé about the influence of Hollywood on our children, Mrs. Randall. That surprises me. I thought you would be more worried — angrier — about a teacher sending our children to R-rated movies. It's like he's *trying* to corrupt them."

"Well, I agree that it shows bad judgment to just do this without first communicating to parents. But worrying about the effect that watching this movie will have on the students just isn't the point. What they watch, what they read — that's not what's going to corrupt them. Corruption comes from a heart that's separated from God, from the darkness of this world and the way it can grind you down. Don't fret over a couple of antiheroes on the big screen — worry about what's happening *inside* our kids, and how we can help them find the kingdom of God. Teach them to love, teach them to heal and to feel God's spirit within themselves, and we'll be doing what we should be doing."

"So are you not going to talk to your husband?" Mrs. Posey asked.

"Oh, I will — and if I know John, he's going to want to have a talk with Mr. Borden. Not because he's an evil influence, but because he needs to think these things through a little better. And I'm sure you're not the only parent who's bothered, so I'm guessing there will be other discussions."

"I'm sure there will," Mrs. Posey said primly, "if I have anything to say about it."

Proper 18 / Ordinary Time 23

Mark 7:24-37

A Matter Of Justice

Laughing Maid sat still as death, listening to the clock as it ticked — a curious sound she had never heard before, somehow maddening and soothing at the same time as it seemed to beat in synchrony with her heart. As she listened, she stared fixedly at the newspaper in her hands, hoping that it would help her blend in, even while she knew it did not. Without looking, she could *feel* the eyes of every woman and child in the room as they searched her out.

The number of women and children had waxed and waned throughout the afternoon, a steady march of patients through the doctor's office, while she waited for her own name to be called. It did not escape her notice that all of the patients going into the doctor's inner office had arrived after her; nor did it escape her notice that at least *some* of them had given her snide, unwelcome looks as they passed by her.

It was a look she was familiar with.

The same look many people gave her when she went into town, on those rare occasions when she needed to leave the reservation; essentially the same look the conductor on the train and the ticket agent, had given her when she embarked on her trip to Chicago, and a close relative to the expression of the owner of the rooming house in which she and her daughter had found themselves.

It was a silent warning to her that she was terribly out of place, and had no business being out among people who were better than her.

Any other day, it might have been enough to send her back to the reservation, but not today… not with so much at stake. Humiliation was a small price to pay for the gift of life, if she could secure it, and she had no intention of squandering it on hurt feelings and wounded pride. Not with her daughter's life at stake.

She almost didn't hear when the woman at the desk called out to her. "Miss… Laughing Maid. I'm afraid Doctor Randall will *not* be able to see you today, after all."

Her heart sank. "But you told me he would see me, once the other patients had been seen." She looked around the room, realized she was the last person waiting. "I will only need a short time with him, I promise." She stood up, took a step toward the desk. "I do need to see him."

The nurse in the starched white uniform looked at her — but *through* her — and said mechanically. "I'm afraid that won't be possible."

"Tomorrow, then?" Laughing Maid proposed. "Will he see me tomorrow?"

The nurse sighed. "You can try, I suppose. We open at nine o'clock, sharp. We can try to fit you in some time. But there are no guarantees."

"Please, I don't think you understand. I came all this way from the reservation at Lac des Morts, and I —"

Before she could finish the door to the inner office opened and a middle-aged man stood in the doorway. "Excuse me, but did you say the Lac des Morts Reservation?"

It took a moment for Laughing Maid to realize he was talking to her, then she nodded eagerly. "Yes, sir. That is where we come from, my daughter and I."

There was a moment of hesitation, then he shook his head slightly and stepped aside, ushering her into the office. As she entered, he looked past her to his nurse. "It's all right, Ingrid."

She looked perplexed. "But, Doctor — she's a... an *Indian*."

"Yes, I know. She's from the reservation where my brother is living."

Her eyes widened. "Your brother is living on —"

The rest was lost when the door closed. Hubert Randall pointed to a straight backed chair in front of his desk, and sat down in a plush leather chair on the other side. "I apologize, it appears you've been waiting a long time, Miss —?"

"My name is Laughing Maid, Doctor. And I have been waiting most of the day."

"Again, I apologize. You're not our usual clientele, and I guess my nurse didn't quite know what to do with you. That being said, what can *I* do for you? What brings you all those hundreds of miles from your home?"

"My daughter, sir — Running Doe. She is eleven years old, and she has something in her stomach. A tumor, I think it's called. It's killing her, and it needs to be taken out. Your brother said that you can do that — that you are what he called a surgeon. You can cut it out with special tools. Is that true?"

He nodded. "Yes, basically. Depending upon what exactly is wrong, I can operate and remove a tumor relatively easily. But —" He hesitated. "I have a pretty busy schedule and the procedure is not inexpensive. I — to be honest — I don't operate on people like you. People without means, I mean," he added hastily. "And I'm not sure the hospital where I work would be... comfortable... admitting... a person like you."

"An Indian, you mean?"

"Well — to be honest, yes. That's exactly what I mean. Don't you have a doctor who visits the reservation? Or isn't there one in Grandeur?"

"We have Doctor Hochstadder, in Grandeur — but your brother said he wouldn't trust Doctor Hochstadder to butcher a cow. He said you were who we need to see."

In spite of himself, Hubert smiled. "I see my brother doesn't hold back on his opinions, yet. Nevertheless, Miss Laughing Maid, you and your daughter are very out of place, here. There's the cost, the recovery time — you would be much better off back in Wisconsin, among your own people, where you would be comfortable."

She considered what he said, then shook her head. "Sir, I spent the day sitting out there, being judged by everyone I saw. I *know* I am out of place, and my daughter will be, too. We are not rich, we are not white, we are not your kind of people. But my daughter is very sick, and Mister Randall — a man I trust — tells me that you can make her well. So the place I am going to be comfortable is right here, where my daughter can be healed. You have many rich clients — maybe you can fit in a poor one?"

Hubert Randall took off his glasses and polished them slowly with his handkerchief, then put them on and squinted a little. "Your daughter — where is she?"

"At the rooming house. I have the street number."

161

"Right. Let's go see her, Miss Laughing Maid. You've made your point." He got up, opened the door enough to say, "Ingrid, get me — get *us* — a buggy. And make a space on my schedule on Friday, for surgery at Saint Mark's — first name 'Running,' last name 'Doe.'" He closed the door without waiting for the response he knew she would have.

Sometimes, you just had to settle on doing the right thing.

Proper 19 / Ordinary Time 24
Mark 8:27-38

Declaration

It was a darker night than usual.

Part of it was the stars, themselves — they seemed to be withholding their light, choosing to hide behind a layer of clouds in deference to the events of the day. Part of it was the combination of unfamiliar surroundings and the lack of lamp light or fire — unfamiliar surroundings because the olive grove in which they found themselves was one they had never visited before, and would not be on anyone's list of where they might be; and they had no lamp or firelight because — well, what was the point in hiding if you're going to betray your location by lighting a fire?

And part of that darkness, truth be told, lay in the hearts of the men who lay beneath the branches of the trees not sleeping, because every time they closed their eyes, some new horror replayed itself in the eyes of the mind. So they lay awake, trying not to remember that which was unforgettable.

"Truth be told," Peter said softly, "I blame myself." His voice was almost a croak, brittle with unwept tears. "I look back, and I think it's my fault," he said into the darkness.

There was no answer, at first, and Peter thought his brother must have found sleep — and was envious. Then he *did* speak, and his voice was just as low. "Funny thing, that," Andrew murmured. "I'm fairly sure you're right."

Peter propped himself up on his elbows, looked to his right out of reflex, without any hope of seeing his brother just a few feet away. "Andrew, this is the part where you disagree with me. 'No, Peter, don't be silly. It's not your fault.' Something like that would be nice."

He could almost hear the shrug. "When you're right, you're right, brother. I think this is your fault. This whole day — the last twenty-four hours — all your fault. This was always going to be the end, after the

Master asked who we thought he was, and you said he was the Messiah. I knew it then, I know it now."

Peter sighed and lowered himself back down, stared toward the unseen sky. "You have a lot to learn about being a supportive brother."

"And you have a lot to learn about knowing when to speak and what to say. You have a problem, Peter — that thing most people have that keeps them from automatically saying whatever comes to mind… you don't seem to have it. Instead, it just pops out of your mouth, and you end up saying things like, 'You're the Messiah, Jesus.' And that is the first link in a chain that ends up here, with our Master dead on a Roman cross."

"Come, Andrew, we all thought it — you know we did."

"Of *course* we all thought it, we could *see* it. He was a miracle worker, a teacher who spoke not like one who had *learned* things but was the source of them. He was surely sent by God to lead us. He *was* the Messiah. It's just that none of us was mad enough to say so out loud. But once it was said, others were bound to hear — and that would eventually find its way back to the temple, and the priests would find a way to enlist the Romans, and it would end badly. Very badly," Andrew murmured, and shivered at just the flash of a memory of what he had seen the day before.

There was a long silence, then, broken only by the sound of night birds going about their business, and bats snapping insects out of the air as they swooped from tree to tree. "We all knew it," Andrew said finally. "And we all knew that the priests and the Romans would kill him, if they could."

"But the Messiah would be a victorious leader," Peter answered. "A glorious leader who would overthrow the unrighteous and bring about a new kingdom of righteousness. We couldn't very well praise and honor him if we didn't acknowledge who he was, could we?"

"No, I suppose not. But you still forged the first link in the chain by calling him the Messiah. And you encouraged him to keep doing what he was doing — to cast caution to the winds and press for justice and righteousness. Being named for who we believed him to be marked him for death." Another silence. "And then it ended this way — with our friend and Master suffocating on the cross, pierced by a Roman spear."

"I never imagined the Messiah's journey would end that way," Peter said. "Dead, with his disciples in hiding."

"It shouldn't have, so now we have to wonder if he was the Messiah at all, or did we misplace our hopes and dreams?"

"He was special," Peter said firmly. "I still believe he was the Messiah — just not the way we thought he would be. And maybe that's what he was trying to teach us, as well. Some of the things he said — they make more sense if you think of it that way. But I don't know where we go from here."

"Wherever we go, when we think about what happened to him, we have to remember that it started with you — just as you said, when you named him to be the Messiah."

"Well — thank you for that, brother. But can I tell you a secret?"

"Another one?"

He looked toward the darkness, and his brother, again. "Yes. When I said I blame myself, I was talking about how I ran — how I denied him. I wasn't even thinking about when I called him Messiah." He looked skyward. "But thanks for that."

Proper 20 / Ordinary Time 25

Mark 9:30-37

Declaration (Part 2)

Andrew sat up when he realized that the sky was starting to get lighter, and the bird calls were changing. He scratched himself and yawned, tried to decide whether he'd actually gotten any sleep. It was hard to say for sure, as the endless cavalcade of horror that played in his mind, showing him flashes of horror and pain, could just as easily been memories as dreams; nothing he saw behind closed eyes was anything he hadn't seen with them open.

Finally deciding it made no difference — he was too awake to sleep now, regardless — he yawned again and stretched, looked over toward his brother. Peter's eyes were closed, his hands clasped over his stomach. He thought for a moment, then reached down to his side, picked up a handful of pebbles. One by one, he began to toss them toward his brother, mostly landing on his chest and stomach. Finally, one hit his folded hands and he stirred, brushed it away. "You awake?" Andrew asked quietly.

Peter's eyelids fluttered, then opened, and his eyes turned toward Andrew. "No, I was sleeping — had a dream that I was being stoned."

"Sounds terrible; good thing you woke up." Andrew pulled his feet back and raised his knees, rested his elbows on them. "You know — what you said last night, about not being able to shake the feeling that you're responsible for what happened to the Master... it made me think."

"It was bound to happen sometime." Peter grunted and closed his eyes.

"I'm serious," Andrew insisted. "It made me think — think about something that's been on my own mind since he was arrested."

"I don't suppose you're going to let me sleep until I ask what that is?"

"Thanks for asking, brother. I was thinking of that day when we were walking to Capernaum, and some of us started to argue about who was the greatest disciple. Do you remember?"

"Jesus asked what you were arguing about — the way Dad always used to ask questions he already knew the answers to." He snickered, then. "And none of you had the guts to answer him."

"Like you said, he already knew. You knew it, we knew it. Why embarrass ourselves more by actually saying it out loud?" Andrew hung his head, closed his eyes. "I remember being ashamed — but what I remember the most is how *disappointed* he looked. He just looked from face to face, with this look of hurt and disappointment... it made me want to cry." He raised his head, opened his eyes. "It *makes* me want to cry."

Peter sat up, then, and shook his head. "Brother, in three years *all* of us disappointed him at some point. You're not special — not you, or anyone else who was foolish enough to have that argument."

"Nevertheless, we totally missed everything he'd been teaching us — or trying to teach us. About humility, and service, and mercy... about putting other people first. Instead we were like a bunch of hungry Samaritans, shoving each other out of the way to get at a piece of bread. And what did the Master say about it?"

"Anyone who wants to be first must be the very last, and servant to them all," Peter answered. "None of us were very good at that."

"And yet he kept trying. He put himself last to the point of death. He said that, too — he *knew* that he was going to die. Die for *us*, Peter."

"Of course he did. I didn't get it, then, but when I saw him... when they came for him in the garden... I finally knew. I saw it in his eyes — scared to death, with this look of utter certainty about everything that was happening. I don't know how, but he knew he was going to die on that cross, and he wanted us to know it, too. I also think he wanted us to understand that it wasn't a defeat for him."

"What do you mean?"

"Since he told us it was going to happen, and he did nothing to avoid it... since he talked about how the first must be last... I think it was all part of his plan."

Andrew nodded. "I think you're right, brother. But to what end?"

"What do you mean?"

"Is it all some kind of weird object lesson about what it means to put yourself last? About what it means to be a servant? Does it mean you submit to being beaten and flayed, then nailed to a cross... to hang there until you choke out your last breath, or get skewered by a Roman pylum?" He made a futile gesture. "There must have been a better way to teach the lesson."

Peter frowned, shrugged. "If I were the Messiah, perhaps I could answer that. But I'm not, and the only person we could ask — the only person who would know — is gone. Dead. So we'll *never* know." He looked up at the sky, where the sun was starting to poke through the leaves of the olive trees. "All we do know is that our friend *and* our Master — our teacher *and* our servant — died yesterday, and today nothing has changed. And tomorrow, the sun will rise — he will still be in the tomb, and *still* nothing will have changed."

"Then what was the point to all this?" Andrew repeated, not knowing that the answer to his question lay with tomorrow's dawn.

Proper 21 / Ordinary Time 26

Mark 9:38-50

Loyal Opposition

"Begging your pardon, Reverend Lee, but the post commander would like to see you in his office after Sunday service." Sergeant Eustice Wayne stood at attention out of habit as he passed along the invitation to Jamison Lee. "You and the Missus — and the baby," he amended, memory jogged by the sight of Elizabeth and Madeline Lee reading a picture book at the table in the kitchen of the visitors' quarters.

Jamison looked at him curiously. "So this is a social call?" He had already made the customary call to the post commander when he arrived — a formality, as the post commander was quite busy and appeared to have no time for idle chit-chat with the visiting circuit pastor. That discussion had led him to assume that Colonel Donnelly planned to have nothing further to do with him during his stay.

And now this.

Wayne looked past him. "Not exactly, sir. He wants to talk to you about a visitor he had yesterday. A minister from St. Croix Falls came by to ask if he could start holding church services at the fort, so Colonel Donnelly wants to talk to you about it." He looked at Jamison, then. "He just thought it might be a more pleasant talk if it was done over Sunday dinner."

"I see. Well, I will tell Libby and we will be happy to meet with the Colonel," he lied — a social nicety, bound by the customs of life on a military post.

"Very good, sir." Sergeant Wayne turned to leave, then turned back. "Speaking plainly, sir, if you please?"

"Of course, speak away — I'm not your superior officer, sergeant. I'm not *anybody's* superior officer anymore."

The sergeant fidgeted with his hat in his hands. "The colonel and I had a discussion about this, given that he knows I come to Sunday service if I'm on post. I told the colonel I didn't think it would be a good

169

idea to get this new minister involved. We already have you coming by every month for divine services, we hardly need someone else doing the same thing."

Jamison smiled. "Is one service a month all you boys need here? Things have changed."

More fidgeting. "It's not that, reverend. It's just that me and the boys know you, and we know you wore that dirty blue shirt back in the war. You may not know what it's like to fight hostiles, but you know what it's like to take the oath and wear the uniform. Don't know that I ever heard another preacher who could say that. Besides, reverend — word is he's *Lutheran.* You know about them, they have all manner of crazy ideas."

Jamison hesitated, aware that he was in tricky territory. "First, sergeant, thank you — I appreciate your kind words. Serving in the army is a special gift and we don't all share it, but just because someone *didn't* serve shouldn't cause you to discount what they have to say. There are plenty of good men in the pulpit who never served that way — and I'll say there are plenty of soldiers I wouldn't want to be getting my theology from, either."

The sergeant gave a little shrug. "No doubt, sir."

"And if the man really turns out to be Lutheran — well, we can't all be perfect." He smiled. "I'm going to tell you a secret, sergeant: for all the hoopla churches in different denominations will make about how different they are, and as much as they try to sell the idea that they're the ones with the whole, complete truth, when you dig down deep… if they're built on the idea that Jesus is the Son of God and our Savior, and that the route back to God lies through him, then they're basically the same. Some of the details are different, of course, but we're all still doing the same work, proclaiming the same message, and if we happen to be trying to save the same people… well, then, maybe we just doubled the odds of actually getting through to them."

Sergeant Wayne's expression showed skepticism. "If you say so, reverend."

Jamison Lee winked. "I do, sergeant — just don't mention it to the bishop, if you don't mind. No need to bother his head with such things."

Proper 22 / Ordinary Time 27

Mark 10:2-16

The New Pastor

"Would you like more potatoes, Reverend Lee?" Mrs. Donnelly asked, half-extending the bowl toward him.

He smiled, patted his stomach. "No thank you, Mrs. Donnelly — we have a long trip ahead of us back to Lac Des Morts, and I'm not sure I'm going to stay awake as it is. Fortunately, the horses know the way."

Elizabeth Lee declined, as well, with a slight wave of her hand. "No thank you." She glanced at her husband. "I'm a little concerned that my driver may not be awake, so I suppose I had better be."

Mrs. Donnelly laughed politely and set the bowl down. At the other end of the table, her husband shifted in his chair and leaned forward. "So, reverend, I wanted you and Reverend Morton to have a chance to meet — he came to us to ask if he could begin holding divine services here at Fort Bellah, and I gave permission. He's going to be starting next month."

Jamison looked directly across the table, then, at the man in the black frock coat, raised his cup of coffee in toast. "Welcome, Reverend Morton. I'm sure you'll find your new flock here to be as attentive and thoughtful as I do."

Morton dabbed at his lips with a linen napkin, nodded. "Indeed, sir, I'm sure I will. I've ministered to soldiers before, out in the Badlands, and I trust these will be no different." He turned toward the woman on his right — a petite, dark haired woman in a plain, white dress — and added, "My wife is looking forward to this new ministry, as well."

She just smiled wanly in response and took a sip of water from a crystal glass, but made no eye contact.

To Jamison, it appeared that her hand trembled slightly.

"So, Reverend Morton, will you be ministering to the indians at Lac Des Morts Reservation, as well? I know Reverend Lee has found it quite rewarding," Mrs. Donnelly said. Her husband shot her a warning look from the other end of the table, and she immediately fell silent for a moment. "Perhaps I've overstated — or am treading on sensitive ground?" she added with a nervous smile and picked up her glass of water then took a sip – and another.

"Not at all, Mrs. Donnelly," Morton answered. "All questions are fair at the dinner table — isn't that right, Reverend Lee?"

"Of course," Jamison agreed, "Although I've generally found it helpful to avoid the subject of politics, as it tends to sour stomachs and friendships."

"Then I shall be especially careful to steer clear of it. After all, the election of such a buffoon, in itself, is enough to sour the strongest stomach."

Jamison eyed the newcomer for a few moments, then spoke softly. "Perhaps the concept of avoiding politics needs to be clarified."

Elizabeth, beneath the table, put her hand on her husband's knee. Clearing her throat, then, she said, "I think Mrs. Donnelly left a question on the table. Will we have the pleasure of seeing you at the reservation, Reverend Morton? Our home would, of course, be open to you, and we would be pleased to let you use the new church." She squeezed Jamison's knee, looked at him innocently. "Wouldn't we, dear?"

"Of course," he agreed. "The mission field at Lac Des Morts is ripe for the harvest, and there is plenty for all to do. Our friends there have had a very difficult time — they've been relocated twice, and are searching for something to believe in, to cling to. Fortunately, we're able to show them what the Lord can mean to them. In the last two years, we've baptized at least a dozen natives, and some of them are helping to teach others in a Bible study. Having another pastor there, even part time, would be a godsend — literally."

"No doubt," Morton said quietly, "no doubt." He paused to take another drink of coffee, dabbed at his lips again and appeared to be focused on the floral centerpiece of the table for several moments. He started to speak, stopped, then looked across the table at Jamison. "I have no doubt that you're quite busy, Reverend Lee. But I find that my own personal calling is a little different. I think it's more important to focus on bringing Jesus to our soldiers. Where he will do the most

Proper 22 / Ordinary Time 27

good."

"I'm not sure I follow you," Jamison said slowly... quite sure that he did.

"Let's be realistic, Lee, you can baptize your friends, as you call them, from now until judgment day, but you're never going to wash the red away — if you know what I mean."

Jamison breathed in deeply through his nose, let it out through his mouth, started to shift in his seat — and was suddenly aware, again, of Elizabeth's hand on his knee. "Enlighten me," he said in a voice that was eerily calm... a voice that a brigade of men, a decade before, had learned was the prelude to a storm.

Morton, for his part, seemed not to notice. "I've made a study of indians, Lee. There are a lot of misconceptions about them, as a breed, but one thing we know for certain is that they are very childlike at their core. Not really capable of mature social interactions — this is why they have such trouble keeping their treaties. They don't understand laws and obligations."

"Funny — I thought the main problem they had keeping their treaties was that we kept changing them. Kind of hard to know what you're obligated to, when the rules can be changed unilaterally by one party."

"And I repeat, it's scientifically proven that they're childlike. You don't keep agreements with your child if it turns out they're not in your best interest, do you?"

"Well — those are called promises, and I think generally keeping promises is a good idea. But you keep calling them childlike —"

"It's well known. They're not capable of really understanding and accepting the Lord, Lee — not really. That's why I wouldn't bother baptizing them if I were you, unless you're just trying to keep score for your bishop, or something."

Jamison took another deep breath, looked at Elizabeth, who took her hand off his knee and gave a little shrug, a discreet nod of her head. She cleared her throat quietly and stood up. "I think I hear our baby crying," she lied, and left the room.

"Reverend Morton," Jamison said quietly, "assuming all you say is true—if they really are childlike — what about Mark 10:14? 'Suffer

173

the little children to come on to me and forbid them not: for such is the kingdom of heaven.' It's obvious that Jesus has no problem with accepting even the childlike — maybe *especially* the childlike — into the kingdom. The ones who haven't been jaded, the ones who still have an innocence of heart that most adults lose… the ones who can approach the Almighty with a sense of awe and wonder that most of us struggle to find. The ones who've never experienced God in the way we have, and are just discovering him now. Jesus *wants* them."

"But —"

"God's kingdom is open to *everyone,* Reverend Morton. And I'm going to be honest, I am torn between praying for your soul — and your congregants — right now, and punching you in the face. I'm pretty sure Jesus wouldn't approve of the latter, so today is your lucky day. But don't count on getting two of them. I wish you good luck and God speed in ministering to the soldiers here at Fort Bellah — but I hope you can do it without poisoning their minds. And unless and until you can come to Lac Des Morts and apologize to the people you've insulted, I really do hope you stay away my friends. It will be better for your face."

He stood up, bowed stiffly to the post commander and his wife. "Colonel Donnelly, Mrs. Donnelly. Thank you for the hospitality. I apologize for my rudeness, it's just — well, arrogance is a dish best served in small portions, and I've had my fill. Good day."

With that, he turned on his heel and left, stopping by the parlor to pick up Elizabeth and the baby. She said nothing while he helped her with her shawl, spoke only when they had left the post commander's quarters. Then, looking at Jamison slyly out of the corner of her eye, all she said was, "'It will be better for your face?'"

"Too much?"

She smiled. "I didn't say that, colonel."

"It was too much," he said, answering his own question. "It's just that I've seldom heard anyone who purports to be a man of God come across as that ignorant." He glanced over his shoulder, as though he might see into the house. "I just hope I haven't talked myself out of a church, here." He sighed. "These men need God, too."

"Don't we all?" Elizabeth asked reasonably, and paused by the side of the buggy, until he could help her mount the step.

Proper 23 / ORDINARY TIME 28

Mark 10:17-31

Rich Man's Burden

RMS Atlantica, the steward assured the passengers, was not sinking; it was experiencing buoyancy challenges brought on by a minor collision with an iceberg — a collision that had, in fact, torn open four watertight compartments on the port side. It was a confluence of circumstances that included high speed, the iceberg's exceptionally low above-surface profile, and the shipyard's slavish pursuit of the lowest bid which, this time, resulted in attaching hull plates to the ship's ribs with counterfeit bolts that had the structural integrity of Silly Putty® when exposed to temperatures lower than 34 degrees… for the record, six degrees *warmer* than the water temperature in the North Atlantic that night.

Despite his professionally cheerful assurances, the liner *was* sinking, and anyone with an ounce of sense knew it. But in typical fashion, parents did not admit it to their children, nor husbands to their wives. Instead, they grudgingly formed up queues to board the lifeboats, each reporting to their assigned station. At each station, a pair of crewmembers assisted the passengers in boarding their assigned boat while a third checked names off a list, all under the watchful, professionally calm eyes of the assigned lifeboat officer.

Third Officer Schaffer, assigned to Lifeboat 10, became aware of a disturbance in the queue, some distance away. With a curt order to one of the crew to "keep them moving," he sought out the source of the disturbance — walking with purpose but not hurrying, for fear that might send the wrong message and incite a panic. What he found, halfway down the queue, brought him up short.

A young man stood, clad in heavy clothing and a winter coat with a scarf wrapped around his neck; a life jacket completing the ensemble. In his right hand he held a suitcase; at his feet were a larger suitcase and a small trunk, which he pushed along with his feet whenever the line moved.

The young man spotted Schaffer as he approached, waved to him with his left hand. "Sir, sir! Over here, sir! Is this the line for Lifeboat 10?"

Schaffer stopped, looked him over. "Yes it is, son."

The young man looked relieved. "Oh, that's good news, I was afraid I might not be in the right place. Is there anything I need to do while I'm waiting in line?"

"Well," Schaffer began, "if you remember the rules —"

"I did," the young man said eagerly. "I followed all the rules. As soon as the lifeboat station alarm sounded, I got dressed in the warmest clothing I had, I put on my life jacket, and I came up to the deck, here, where I've been waiting, doing everything anyone's told me to do." He looked at Schaffer hopefully. "Is there anything else I need to do to make sure I'm ready for the lifeboat?"

"Yes, there is," Schaffer said crisply. "All this stuff —" He nudged the trunk with his foot. "— you have to leave it behind. Better yet, open it up and hand out any clothes you have to the other people in line, to help them keep warm. You're not going to make it onto the boat — and you're not going to *live* — if you try to hold onto everything you've got. It all has to go — suitcases, trunk, everything. Your possessions are just going to hold you back."

The young man looked crestfallen. "But I followed the rules. I did what I was supposed to do."

Schaffer raised his voice to be heard over the ship's whistle, suddenly blowing to vent steam from the boilers. "If you really want to do what you're supposed to do, don't try to take this stuff with you — give it away, and abandon whatever won't to help one of your fellow passengers." The whistle stopped, then, just as suddenly, and he lowered his voice. "It's really simple — there's no place for your possessions, and they're not important, anyway. So leave them. Hand them out."

The young man looked down at the deck, then up at the sky, and answered — not with words, but by shoving his suitcase and trunk with his foot and taking himself out of queue. Schaffer watched as he maneuvered himself and his belongings away from the queue, finally passing from sight in the darkness.

"Well," Schaffer sighed, "I guess that's one seat we won't be filling."

Proper 24 / Ordinary Time 29

Mark 10:35-45

Rich Man's Privilege

Ninety minutes after the lights went out, it was no longer possible to pretend that *RMS Atlantica* had not been damaged catastrophically — perhaps mortally. The fine teak decks were sloping to port, so much to the point that the list of the ship would soon make it impossible to lower boats on the starboard side, and difficult to board them on the port as they swung further and further away from the lifeboat deck.

Below decks, the president of Atlantic Central Bank & Trust considered the problem as he handed out life jackets to a seemingly endless stream of third and fourth class passengers who had come boiling up from the bowels of the ship in a panic, driven by the common fears of drowning and darkness, with a helping of claustrophobia on the side. A lone steward had been there to try to stem the tide and calm them down, but the president took over when he sniffed the scent of panic in the air.

His face was a recognizable one on *either* side of the Atlantic. That and the demeanor of a man who was used to giving orders and getting people to behave as he wanted them to, had helped him restore some sense of order, if not calm. The steward continued to hand out life jackets and lanterns, and the president distributed them with the aid of his secretary.

Fifth Officer Eckhardt found them thus engaged when he came down to check after no one answered the call from the bridge. He watched for a minute or so, then gently took the president's arm. "Sir, I think you should come with me. Your man, here, should be able to finish handing these out for you."

The banker gently, but firmly, shrugged off the fifth Officer's hand and said, "Don't be silly, Eckhardt. I'm doing perfectly well here — it seems I found a task equal to my abilities."

Eckhardt looked past him at the line of passengers. There were men, women, and children, all with the vaguely unclean look of third and fourth class passengers — a natural consequence of limited lavatory facilities and rationed fresh water. Though most were dressed in street clothes, he estimated that all of their garments added together would not have cost as much as the Saville Row suit the president was wearing... and getting dirty. "No doubt you have, sir, but this is not your place. We have our steward, Mister Rothgar, and your assistant, here, to hand out emergency supplies."

"Indeed, then what would there be for me to do? Go up on deck and stand in line? I can make myself useful here —" He lowered his voice, looked at Eckhardt in the faint glow of emergency lighting. "— where I may be able to help keep people from drowning."

Eckhardt considered what his superior officer would have to say to that and shook his head. "I'm afraid I must insist, sir."

The president raised an eyebrow, then turned back to face the next person in line, hand them a life jacket with brief but clear instructions for use. "I encourage you to look at this reasonably, Mister Eckhardt," he said quietly, his voice pitched to the ship's officer's ears. "If your purpose is to save my life, I will tell you now that I have come to the realization that if I am to spend the last minutes of my life on this ship, I would rather spend them actually doing some good for someone. And if I am to survive, I don't want it to come at the cost of leaving these people when I could have stayed to help them."

"Sir —" Eckhardt said uncertainly.

"Tell you what, Mister Eckhardt — if you want to do something really useful, go find your captain and suggest to him that he start flooding a couple of compartments on the starboard side, to see if we can even out our list as *Atlantica* settles in the water. That will allow the most lifeboats to be launched." The fifth Officer just stared back, and the president nodded to show that he was serious. "I mean it, Mister Eckhardt. I've no intention of leaving these people, but if you can talk the captain into equalizing our list, that will save some souls tonight." He smiled. "And *that* will be a task that could reasonably distract you from trying to drag an old banker up to a lifeboat."

Without another word, Fifth Officer Eckhardt spun and elbowed his way up the ladder.

For the next several minutes they worked in relative silence, broken only by hasty instructions. As the number of passengers dwindled, the president's secretary looked at his employer and said, "Sir — may I ask a question?"

"Of course, Roscoe."

"All this — not that you were ever a *bad* employer, sir, but where did *this* come from?"

"When the steward came around right after the collision — and he told us, as a precaution, to get dressed in warm clothes and report to the lifeboat station..." He hesitated. "I followed him out into the passage, and I realized something. He wasn't knocking on every stateroom door. And we know there were no empty staterooms, so he was obviously just going to warn certain people, first. And I'm sure that was his job. But that just rubbed me the wrong way."

He paused again, this time staring into space, not moving until the spell was broken by one of the passengers taking the life jacket out of his hand. "I guess, maybe, divine service got to me yesterday — you know, when the minister was saying that whoever would be great must be a servant. I never did that. Except for a year spent working for the druggist when I was a child, I never served anybody — I made some good guesses about how to invest during the Panic of '73, and some better ones during the Panic of '93, and I came out of it owning a bank... but over the last couple years, I started to get the feeling that *it* owned *me*. And then I heard the minister, yesterday, and I thought: people think being rich makes me a great man — but now I know what makes a man *truly* great is a willingness to humble himself to serve others. And truth be told, it *is* a good feeling — one I've actually earned."

His secretary grunted. "If you don't mind me saying so, sir, you seem to have a talent for it."

The president smiled. "I do, don't I? I kind of hope this isn't a one night thing." He tried to decide if the deck was sloping more, decided he couldn't tell. "Speaking of that, I think it's high time you went up, Roscoe — you and Mr. Rothgar. We're almost done, here, and I can handle it myself." He paused, licked his lips with a quick motion, tried to keep his voice cheerful. "You go up to our station and save me a seat. I'll be along shortly."

The discussion was short, and Roscoe could not break the habit of doing what the president told him to do; he left and took the steward with him. The president took care of the rest of the passengers cheerfully, and when the last one had disappeared up the ladder, he looked around with a sense of satisfaction. He waited just a moment or two, then grabbed the last couple unused life jackets and began to climb the ladder to the next deck.

He was partway up when he stopped to look down into the darkness... was that water he heard, flowing into the passageway?

Proper 25 / Ordinaray Time 30

Mark 10:46-52

The Darkness

You asked me a question, but before I answer it, I need you to do something for me.

Call it a favor, call it an experiment, call it what you will, but I need you to do one thing so that you can understand what I'm going to tell you.

Will you do it for me?

I want you to go outside — go to the nearest market. Can you do that? Good. Now, once you're there, I want you to sit down, close your eyes as tightly as you can, and then put your hands over them, just to make sure no light gets through. Once you've done that, I want you to sit back and listen.

Just listen.

Don't think about what it looked like the last time you saw that market. Don't think about any market you've *ever* seen. Instead, I want you to try to experience the market by sound and smell only. I'm sure it's tempting to cheat and think about what you saw when you were there, but don't. For just a few minutes, live in a world of sound, taste, and touch. If you're feeling brave, you can get up and walk around — but keep those eyes shut!

How does it feel? Awkward, right?

And yet, no matter how hard you try not to, you can't help but think about the last time you saw it. You use sight to build a model of the market in your head, and it stays there. Try to imagine never seeing the sky, or a rainbow, or a child's face — *anybody's* face — try to imagine never looking up at the magnificence of the temple, with your heart breaking at the beauty of it all.

You're imagining *my* world.

I don't know if I was born blind, or just struck blind so young that I can't remember anything but darkness, but that was the world I lived in for years. People — well-meaning people, I think — will say that you can't really miss something if you never had it or never experienced it in the first place, but I can tell you with dead certainty that they are wrong. I can't tell you how old I was, but I was just a child when I first realized that other people *could* see — that there was even such a thing as seeing — and once I knew, I desperately wished that I could see, too.

I could sit for hours and listen to my parents, or my brother and sisters, talk about what they saw, describe the magnificence of a rainbow or the beauty of a crescent moon hanging in the sky, surrounded by stars. It filled me with joy, just to know such things existed outside of the darkness that imprisoned me — but it also filled me with frustration, knowing that I could never really experience them the same way as everyone else.

Instead, I had to be content to sit and listen to a world I would never see.

And then, one day, I heard some travelers talking about this man — this Galilean rabbi that people said could make the lame walk and the blind see, and I began to wonder: could he really do that? Could he really give sight to someone like me, poor, blind Bartimaeus from Jericho?

It was a fantasy I lived almost every day after that. Almost every day I would dream about encountering the Galilean and then having my vision given to me in a thunderous burst of light and color. And every day, I would find myself at the end of the day still in darkness.

Every day, because I knew it might be *possible*, my longing for the light grew stronger.

And then, one day, sitting by the side of the road, I heard a commotion. Then I heard voices that I could pick out of the commotion. And *then* I heard someone say, "There he is! It's Jesus!"

I jumped to my feet and began to shout, "Jesus! Son of David! Heal me! Jesus, have mercy! Jesus, heal me!" Others around me tried to shush me, but I wouldn't have it. I just kept crying out, "Jesus! Heal me!" but my voice was drowned out by a hundred others, all seeking to be cured of one thing or another, and my heart began to sink as it seemed like the crowd noise was starting to recede. Then I shouted — I pleaded — one more time, "Jesus, bring me light!"

And even as I said it there was an electricity in the air, like a bolt of lightning about to strike. The crowd seemed to go silent, and I heard one voice say, "Bring him to me," and my heart leapt! Then there were other voices, suddenly, calling for me to be brought to him — I imagine those were his disciples. Men in the crowd took me by the arm and led me toward where he had spoken, then we stopped, and I trembled.

"What would you like me to do for you?" a voice asked from the darkness.

"Let me see," I said, my voice quivering. "Let me see the light,"

I swear to you that I could *hear* him smile, and he said, "Go. Your faith has made you well."

And then, all glory to God, I could *see* him smile! Suddenly I could see, and the first sight for these eyes was Jesus, smiling at me as light suddenly came into my life. Then, without another word, he moved on — and left me to soak in the world in a way I'd never dreamt would happen.

I tell you, experiencing the light was like experiencing life... it was like I was suddenly connected to the world in the way I should be. And to answer your question, *that's* why I follow him now. After a lifetime in darkness, he brought the light to me, and life will never be the same. I don't know where this journey ends, but as long as we journey in light, I will be there.

Proper 26 / Ordinary Time 31

Mark 12:28-34

Teacher's Pet

Samuel hung up his cloak and poured himself a cup of water from the jug on the table. Eli looked up from the scroll he was meticulously copying, and placed a finger on the original to hold his place. "You missed dinner," he said without preamble. "You never miss dinner. Are you sick?"

"I'm sick and tired, if that counts," Samuel answered, then elaborated. "I was out walking, and lost track of time. I'm sorry."

Eli shrugged. "More food for the rest of us." He used his foot to push out a stool, patted the table with his hand. "Come sit down with me, Samuel, and tell me what's going on." Without waiting for a response, he rolled up the original scroll he was copying and the duplicate he had been working on put them in a cubbyhole, recessed in the wall behind the table.

Samuel sat down but said nothing.

"So talk to me," Eli pressed after a short silence. "What's going on?"

"It's that suck-up Ruben. He invited me to go with him, to see that Galilean that's been making so much trouble."

"Jesus, yes — we've had our eye on him, of course. So what happened?"

"I already said it: Ruben is a suck-up. A teacher's pet. A kiss —"

Eli raised a hand. "Enough. I understand. He has always been an excellent student, Samuel, that's why we asked him to pay particular attention to the Galilean."

"I think he's forgotten why he's there. He's been following the Galilean around for months, absorbing everything he's said. Today, while we were there listening to him teach his disciples, Ruben decided to ask a question. He got up and asked him, 'Jesus — which of the commandments is most important?'"

Eli nodded. "A good question for the country bumpkin, Samuel.

Lord knows it's been the subject of discussion among *educated* men. It would be a good chance to trip him up."

"That's just it — I don't think Ruben was trying to trip him up. I think he truly wanted to hear how Jesus would answer the question."

That caused Eli's brow to furrow. He was silent for a couple of moments, then mumbled, "Still, it was a good question. What did the Galilean say? Something ridiculous, I hope?"

"He said the first is that 'the Lord our God is one, and we should love the Lord with all our heart, all our soul, all our mind, and all our strength.' And then he said the other most important commandment is 'you should love your neighbor as yourself. No other commandment is as great as these.' His words."

"Oh my. And what did Ruben say to that?"

"He rolled over, Eli. He sold out completely. He said, 'You're right, Rabbi — and remembering this is much more important than all the burnt offerings and sacrifices we do.'"

"Oh my," Eli repeated. "That's not good. That's not good at all."

"You're telling me! It's like Ruben is spitting on everything we do — everything that happens at the temple, everything we try to teach the people. We have a place in this society, and he is just throwing it away."

"Now, Samuel, Ruben is a good man. I'm sure he didn't mean it that way."

"How he meant it and how he said it are two different things, then, because Jesus basically patted him on the head and told him he was a good boy. It was disgusting to hear this bumpkin from Galilee talk down to a *scribe* that way, and even more disgusting to watch him accept the praise as though it meant something."

"Did you challenge him?"

"Well — no. Ruben answered properly, we know that. I think I've heard you say virtually the same thing, yourself. But to have him bandy about the law with this no-account nobody is something else entirely. I wanted to punch him, but I figured that would not show proper decorum."

Eli smiled faintly. "Not in front of witnesses, it wouldn't. So what did you do?"

"I left. I didn't know what else to do. I left, and I walked, and I stewed about it... then I came here."

"I see." The old scribe frowned, then. "I think our brother has been spending too much time with the Galilean. Sometimes that can cause a person to lose perspective. He needs some time to regain it — I can find him something to do here, to occupy his mind and ward off distractions." He turned and glanced at the niches in the wall behind him, then added thoughtfully, "The synagogue in Corinth has requested a copy of the law. It might do our brother well to spend some time doing that for them."

"If you can find him."

"What do you mean?"

"I mean the last time I saw him, he was following after the Galilean, like some moon-eyed girl chasing after a boy. I'm not sure he was planning to come home."

"Oh," Eli said slowly, "now that *is* a problem. We can't have our people doing that, can we? Do you know where the Galilean is now?"

Samuel shrugged. "He's not hard to find — just look for a crowd of simpletons, and he's sure to be nearby."

"Then get a good night's sleep, and tomorrow I want you to find him — find Ruben — and talk some sense into him."

"That might not be easy to do."

Eli stood up, then, and picked up a rag, wiped his hands with it and dropped it on the table. "I don't care if it's easy — I just want it done."

"As you wish, Eli," Samuel answered.

But Eli was already leaving the room.

All Saints' Day

John 11:32-44

The Promise

Pack forty men into a room during a Florida summer, without air conditioning and next to no ventilation, add in the aroma of sweaty sheets, uncollected bedpans, and the subtle bouquet of vomit, and it would approximate the conditions in the typhoid ward of the base hospital outside of Jacksonville. Hubert Randall did not have a weak stomach — as a physician, he could not afford that luxury — but as he walked onto the ward, his stomach flipflopped and threatened to rise up; he forced it down with grim determination.

He stood for a moment, eyes narrowed in the dim light, trying to pick out faces in the two long rows of beds. After a moment or two he approached the one man who was up and walking, an orderly in a lab coat that was encrusted with blood, pus, and other less savory stains. "Corporal Mason Randall?" he inquired.

The orderly pointed toward the far end of the room. "Down there, second from the end on the right."

"Thank you." He let the slightly dazed looking young man go back to his tasks, and walked down toward the end of the row. His eyes swept the faces of the men who lay in the beds — some asleep or unconscious, others awake and muttering to themselves; these were restrained to their beds by ropes. A few tried to meet his eyes and nod a welcome, but he did nothing but the slightest of nods in return.

When he reached the second bed from the end, he stopped at the foot of it and studied the patient — Mason Randall. His hands were shriveled and his skin was sallow, his eyes were fixed on the ceiling. But then something — who knew what — told him he had a visitor, and he turned them toward Hubert without moving his head. "Hubert?" he croaked, "is that you?"

Hubert placed a hand on his brother's covered leg. "Yes, Mason. I heard you decided to take some time off from this damn fool soldiering that you signed up for, so I wanted to come see you. How are you feeling?"

There was a raspy chuckle. "Feeling kind of poorly, truth be told. My temperature this morning was a hundred and four. They gave me something to drink, if I get thirsty — but I'm not."

Hubert's eyes flickered toward the glass on the stand next to the bed. Someone had given him milk, but after hours in the heat of the day it was starting to separate, with the top a layer of yellowish fat that floated on an off-white base. Flies congregated around the glass, some clinging to the walls inside, others daring to land on the surface of the contents. "I think we need to get you some water," he said, and started to look around for the orderly.

"Water's contaminated," Mason answered. "That's why they're spending the money on milk."

"I'm not sure they're doing you any favors."

His brother shrugged. "Doesn't much matter, I'm not long for this world anyways."

Hubert started to disagree — then hesitated, and said quietly, "I'm afraid you might be right."

"I've seen enough typhoid in the last two months — I know."

"I wish I could have gotten here sooner, little brother. When I got the telegram, I had to put my practice in order before I could leave."

"Don't worry, big brother. There's nothing you could have done." He shook his head. "After the *Maine*, when I signed on with the First Wisconsin — I had a feeling. But I thought I would die on a hill in Cuba, or landing in the Philippines — not puking out my life in a hospital in Florida."

"Why'd you do it, man? You've got a wife and a child. Madeline couldn't have been happy about you enlisting."

"She understood. She looked up to her father for his service back in the war, she knew what would call a man to serve his country." He paused, took a ragged breath. "But I do wish George would have been old enough to remember me. he'll never have any idea."

"I'll make sure he does — and Madeline will, too," his brother promised. "You know we will. She wanted to come down herself, but with George it would have been too long a trip."

"I wouldn't have wanted him — either of them — to see me like this. Let them have happy memories." His eyes fluttered and closed for a few moments; when he opened them again, they drooped. His breathing was more labored, his speech coming in short bursts between breaths. "I'm not feeling right, Hubert. It's — I can't quite describe it." He took a deep breath, then another. "It's not right."

Hubert licked his lips, closed his eyes and took a deep breath. "I know. Don't think about it, little brother. Just rest. Would you like me to read you something?"

There was a long pause. "Read to me from John," he said finally, his voice very soft. "Read me my favorite part. You know what it is." He glanced toward the stand next to the bed. "The Bible is in the drawer. It's John 11."

"I know," Hubert said quietly, opening the drawer. He pulled out the dogeared Bible and began flipping through the pages.

"It's Lazarus. The story of Lazarus."

"I know," Hubert repeated. "You used to talk about it all the time. You thought it would be interesting to die and come back like he did."

"Still do, but I know it won't be like that. It took me a long time to realize… that Jesus didn't raise Lazarus… because he was a friend. He did it to show God had power over death. Did it to show… why the grave couldn't hold him. People think this is about a miracle… but it's about a promise. God's promise." He took a couple of deep breaths, plunged on. "And now he doesn't have to show it anymore… he came back… so we can die in peace… and not get disturbed once we're gone."

Hubert found the right page, cleared his throat.

"But do me a favor, big brother?"

"Anything," Hubert promised.

"Tell her I was brave… and I know we'll all be raised up one day… to be together."

"Of course." Hubert hesitated, then leaned over the bed and kissed his brother gently on the forehead — felt the heat and the sweat, but didn't care. "You *are* brave, little brother — the bravest man I've ever met." He looked down at the Bible, had trouble focusing on the words.

"But let's read this again — one more time and remember the promise."

And, quietly, he began to read his brother into the darkness... and the light.

Proper 27 / Ordinary Time 32

Mark 12:38-44

The Widow

Jamison Lee looked up at the house number, checked it against the paper in his hand, and frowned. In its day — a decade or so ago — it might have been a modest little house, the sort of place that had a perfect white picket fence, painted shutters, and a neat garden in the front. Those days had slipped away, as they often did in the city; now the fence was missing pickets, a couple of the shutters hung askew and were missing slats, and the paint was flaking. The garden, incongruously, was still neatly kept.

Jamison let himself in — there was no latch on the gate — and walked up to the house, knocked on the door and listened. When a minute went by with no response, he knocked again, a little louder, and said, "Mrs. Stoltz? It's Pastor Lee. Have you got a minute?" As he spoke, he used a hand to shield the window from glare and peered into the gloomy interior.

"One minute," a voice answered almost right away. There was the sound of slow steps on a hardwood floor, then, and the voice repeated, "One minute, pastor."

"Take your time," he answered, and looked around at the exterior again.

She was as good as her word — it was nearly a minute before she reached the door and opened it, pausing first with it part-way open, so she could see who was there, before opening it wide. "Pastor, what a nice surprise! What can I do for you?" she asked, in the tone of voice most people had when the pastor showed up unexpectedly — as though they should be hiding something, but they didn't know quite what.

He bent down, slightly, so he was closer to eye level, and took her hand, shook it gently. "I wondered if you would have a minute to speak to me, Mrs. Stoltz?"

"Is there something wrong?"

"No, no, nothing like that. I just —" he lowered his voice. "It's about your offering."

She looked outside, in both directions, then stood back and beckoned for Jamison to enter. She closed the door after him and led him to the parlor. "Would you like some tea, pastor? Or cookies?" she asked and gestured for him to have a seat. He waited until she sat down, then sat quickly.

"No thank you, I won't be long," he answered. "As I mentioned, I wanted to have a word with you about your offering."

She looked distressed. "I know. We got used to doing things a certain way when Mr. Stoltz was with us, but since he's passed, I'm afraid I haven't been able to keep up with what we'd like to do." She fidgeted. "I'm sorry."

"Don't be," Jamison said gently, "I'm here because — well, this is embarrassing. You know Mr. Heinz, from the bank, is one of our money counters. He saw your offering, and he noticed that your offering this week… well, it was everything you had left in your savings account. You withdrew it and gave it to the church. I have to be honest, Mrs. Stoltz, I'm not comfortable with that."

She looked at him curiously. "Pastor Lee, I'm confused. Didn't you preach a sermon on the widow's mites? The woman who gave her last two coins to the temple?"

"I did."

"And haven't you talked about sacrificial giving?"

"I have."

"Then I don't understand."

"Mrs. Stoltz, your faith is admirable — but part of the church's mission is to see to it that the poor and the vulnerable are taken care of. It's what Jesus has called us to do. And I think part of that includes making sure that *you*, in your generosity, do not put yourself in a vulnerable position. I would not want you to go hungry or be unable to provide the basic necessities of life because you gave to the church." He paused. "If you remember the reading from Mark, it would be a little too much like the officials at the temple 'devouring the widows' houses.'"

"Then why did Jesus make such a fuss over the widow?"

"I think we have to look at it in the context of what he's preached all along: service to the kingdom of heaven not out of a place of power, but a place of humility. Giving not because we have the money, but because we recognize whatever we do have comes from God — and being willing to give that all up, if need be. Just as Jesus did. On the night he was arrested, Jesus was as powerless and vulnerable as a human being could be — but he used that very vulnerability to change the world."

"I'm confused," she said fretfully.

"I don't blame you. These are conflicting messages, and we have to read them in the context of what was going on, what was just said — even what's coming next. But let's keep it simple. Your faith is astounding — but I'm pretty sure Jesus would not want you to go hungry, or even end up having to leave your home just to support the mission of the church — because part of the mission is to watch over widows and orphans."

He reached into the inner pocket of his coat, pulled out an envelope and handed it to her. "Twenty-seven dollars and eighty cents," he said. "Basically everything you have in the whole world. Please do me the favor of taking it back, and then giving what you can afford — while keeping your own body and soul together."

She took the envelope, clasped it in both hands. "Please tell Mr. Heinz thank you," she said softly. "I was wondering where dinner was going to come from — and now I know."

"Grace and generosity flow both ways," Jamison said. "Remember that. And don't lose your passion for being all in — just find a way to do it that embraces God's grace for you, too."

Proper 28 / Ordinary Time 33

Mark 13:1-8

Apocalypse

Madeline Randall heard the screen door in the kitchen slam shut, hastily folded the *"The Milwaukee Socialist Courier"* and set it aside before her son made it to the dining room. He stopped at her chair, dutifully let her kiss him on the forehead. "How was school, George?" she asked brightly. "Did you have your spelling test?"

He shrugged. "Yeah, we did. It was Ok."

"And?"

"Got a 99." He scowled. "I got prestidigitation wrong — used an 'e' instead of an 'i.'"

She looked surprised. "Was that even on your list?"

"Teacher does what she calls a surprise word every week. It's usually from something she read to us." His eyes drifted past her, to the folded newspaper on the table; his brow furrowed. "What's that mean — 'West Coast Apocalypse?'"

"It means —"

As she answered, he picked up the paper, unfolded it so he could read the front page. "'West Coast Apocalypse. Thousands Feared Dead in City by the Bay.' What are they talking about?"

Madeline sighed, wistfully wondered what it would be like to have an average second grade reader. "There was a big earthquake in San Francisco yesterday, George. It was — pretty bad."

"Thousands of people were killed?" His eight-year-old face was intensely serious.

"It looks that way," his mother answered. "They won't know until after the fires are out," she added, and instantly regretted adding that detail. George had an extraordinary imagination, and it was all too easy to believe that he could — in some way — imagine what it would be like to have a whole city burning.

Her son absorbed that information quietly, then briefly looked upward before turning his eyes back to her. "Do you think this is — you know — the beginning of the end?"

She blinked. "You mean the end of the world?"

He nodded. "Like Jesus said — there are going to be earthquakes, wars and rumors of wars. Famines — and then the end comes. Grandpa talks about it — it's in the Bible," he added helpfully. He glanced up again. "Do we have to be ready?"

"Well — I'm pretty sure your Grandpa Lee would say that we should *always* be ready. But —" she hesitated, not sure that was the path to take, "if you remember, he also said that these are things that have been with us throughout history. And Jesus, when he was talking — well, a lot of it had to do with what was going to happen to his disciples, and to the Jewish people when the Romans ended their rebellion. He was warning his disciples more about the immediate future — and then about what would happen many, many years from then, or from now."

"So the end of the world *isn't* coming?"

"I don't think this is a sign, George. There are earthquakes every year. Every year, somewhere, someone is struck by famine. And as far as wars —" She hesitated. "If there's an apocalypse, I'm afraid it's of our own doing. Human beings have a talent for war and destruction, and it only seems to get worse the smarter we get."

"Daddy died in the war, right?"

Another pause. "Yes, he did — he got sick. But he signed up to be in the army because he thought he would be helping to set people free. That's what heroes do, and your Daddy was a hero."

In its own way, Mason's death had been the end of *her* world — but George had been the reason she kept going, and maybe one day she could share that, but not now. Instead, she sighed and reached out to take her son's hand. "No doubt, Jesus will come back some day to bring us all to heaven — but no one knows when that will be, and anyone who tries to tell you they know… that they can point to what's happening in the world and tell you the time is coming soon… they're wrong."

He looked at her, his brain working behind his gaze.

"Some days I think it would be nice to know," she added, "but then others I think, why? The point is to live a good life, a Christian life, now, so whenever it happens we'll be ready."

"So — 'wars and rumors of wars?'" George asked uncertainly.

She squeezed his hand. "Georgie — I'm sorry, but I'm pretty sure you're going to see natural disasters over time, and plenty of wars as you grow up — and it won't mean the end is near. It will just mean that, sometimes, human beings sell their souls cheap."

George looked at his mother gravely and could think of nothing to say — so he put his arms around her neck and lay his head on her breast.

#

Sergeant George Mason Randall stood on the parapet and looked out at the moonscape of No Man's Land, a nightmare of charred, twisted trees, craters, and miles of barbed wire, lit by the intense white light of phosphorus shells that were a passable imitation for the fires of hell. Any minute now the whistles would blow, and men — by the thousands — would come swarming out of their trenches and throw themselves across that landscape.

One by one, a thousand worlds would end, though the planet kept turning.

He sighed and murmured. "Oh, Mom... you had no idea how right you were...."

Reign of Christ / Proper 29 / Ordinary Time 34

John 18:33-37

The Truth

"What do you suppose the truth is?"

Iunio considered the question as he burnished his helmet with a strip torn from the tunic of one of the criminals who had died that day — *the mad preacher*, he thought, but he could not be sure; he had been fortunate enough to win several rounds of lots cast for the dead men's belongings. He breathed on one particular and spot buffed it until the spot faded.

He set the helmet on the shelf, turned to Marcus, who had asked the question. "The truth is my feet are tired and my arms hurt — and I may have thrown my shoulder out when I broke that last thief's knees during the crurifragium." He placed a hand on his shoulder, rolled it forward a couple of times, flexing his forearm. "It hurts like a son-of-a-gun. Does that ever happen to you?"

"Happens when you swing too hard — you swing like you're hitting *through* the knees, and then it's like you end up hitting the cross, too. You may as well be hitting a wall."

"So I have to ease up?"

Marcus nodded. "Yeah — if it means you have to take a couple of whacks at each knee, it's still better for your shoulder. You'll thank me next time."

"I'll thank you now — that sounds like good advice."

"But the state of your sorry, arthritic body is not what I was talking about. I wonder what that Jew prophet was talking about when he said he was here to testify to the truth."

"You don't know?"

"Know what?"

"The 'truth' he was testifying to. You don't pay attention to what people are talking about, do you?"

"They're Jews — and barbarians. Slave bait and arena fodder. Why should I listen to anything they have to say?"

"Then why do you care what the Galilean was talking about?"

"Because Pilate piqued my interest. He talked to him like he was a rational person. So I wonder just what it is he thinks he came to testify to."

"Oh, nothing much, just that he is — or was — the son of a god. That their temple was going to be completely destroyed, but that he would rebuild it himself in three days. That he was here to bring peace and justice, and to save people from their own sins."

"I thought these people had some crazy one-god thing going?"

"They do — they believe there is only one god, and that they worship him. But — come on, does that make any sense? How could one god run an entire world — but you're right. He believes he's the son of *the* god."

"And the temple — are you making that up?"

"No, I heard it from a guy who heard it from a guy. He said you can destroy this temple, but he will raise it up in three days." He snorted. "It took their King Herod decades to finish; some handyman from Galilee is not going to pull it off in three days."

"So when you call him crazy —?"

Iunio nodded. "He really was. He believed the whole world was sinful — that everybody in it were sinners, and everyone was condemned to death, and only *he* could save them."

"How could he do that?"

"I don't know, but I heard that him getting arrested and sent to the cross was part of it. I guess — and this is just what I heard — I guess he was kind of like a sacrifice? You know, the way normal people will sacrifice a sheep, or a bull — he took it that extra step. That's why he never really defended himself in front of Pilate — he *wanted* to be condemned, because that was the only way he believed he could take on everybody's sins." The Romans don't really believe what Jesus is doing at this moment in time.

"But even if that's true, how does that help? People are just going to sin again... I mean, by their way of looking at things."

"I know. But he told his followers that anybody who believed in him — and I guess that means believing he was a demigod, and a sacrifice —

anybody who believed would be saved. Going forward, too." He shook his head. "Crazy, right?"

"So everybody's just supposed to take his word for it? Now that he's dead, they're saved?"

Iunio looked around to be sure they were alone, then lowered his voice. "I heard this from a centurion who was stationed in Capernaum last year. Jesus evidently really *could* heal some people — he healed this centurion's servant. And he must have figured he could do it for himself, too, because Jesus said the proof of everything he said would be that he would rise from the grave on the third day."

"Get out!"

"I know, right? But that's what he said. And I'll tell you, he had this centurion half-convinced he could do it."

Marcus looked thoughtful. "Is *that* maybe what he was talking about when he said he could raise up the temple in three days?"

Iunio shrugged. "Who knows? He did love his metaphors. But I can tell you this: he's not rising on the third day, or the thirtieth, or in the third hour. That man is dead — when I stuck my spear in him, there was no heartbeat, just the spray of blood and fluid that had accumulated in his chest to smother him. And when they took him down, there was no breath nor bleeding. So if rising from the grave was the truth he came to testify to, he was wasting his time."

Marcus sighed and shook his head. "You have to wonder how someone gets to be that crazy."

"I don't," Iunio said shortly. When his friend looked at him curiously, he added, "Think of it, Marcus — out here in this wasteland of ignorance… away from civilization. How do more of these people *not* go crazy?"

Both men laughed, then, and Iunio was starting to change out of his armor when there was a voice in the hall. "Iunio!" There were footsteps, then a short man appeared in the doorway. "Iunio! I hope you haven't gotten comfortable."

"What now?" he answered, automatically reaching for his sword and helmet.

"Pick a squad and grab some rations. You're going on extra duty."

"What's that?" he asked, buckling his belt and sword.

"Security detail. You and the men are to go out and guard that Galilean's tomb — make sure he stays in it." The clerk turned around, started to leave.

"Wait! Have you gone crazy, too?" Iunio demanded.

The clerk turned back to him, rolled his eyes. "Not me, centurion — Pilate. The priests came to him with some wild claims the Galilean made. He wants to be sure no one steals the body and claims his prophecies have come true. But cheer up — there's extra duty pay for this. Easiest money you'll ever make."

"Well, I can't argue with that. How long?"

The clerk shrugged. "Just through Sunday. Once the priests and scribes have come out to certify he's still in the tomb, we should be Okay."

"Sunday it is," Iunio agreed, and put on his helmet. "And you're right about one thing — it's the easiest money I'll ever make." They all laughed at that.

They wouldn't be laughing Sunday morning...

Thanksgiving Day

Matthew 6:25-33

What's For Dinner?

"Did you ever see *Alive*?"

She didn't look up, just continued to open cabinet doors methodically. What?

"It was a movie, back about forty years ago — true story, about a Venezuelan soccer team that crashed in the mountains in Peru."

She shook her head and sighed. "Dude — it was about a rugby team from Uruguay, and the plane crashed in Argentina. Did *you* see it?"

He shrugged. "I was ten, I didn't catch all the details. Dad rented it for my tenth birthday party — a sleepover."

She grunted and went back to searching kitchen cabinets. "Was Blockbuster out of *Silence of the Lambs*?" she asked, peering into the cabinet next to the oven. She reached in, pushed some pots and pans around, pulled out a canister.

"You know, that's the same thing Mom asked him. I couldn't hear his answer through the door."

"Good times. Why'd you bring it up?" She shook the canister, opened it, tossed it aside. It clattered on the tile floor.

"You know what happened, right?"

She scanned the cabinet again, with a flashlight, then stooped down to look in the cabinet under the counter. "Make your point," she answered.

"They ended up eating one of their teammates, because they were starving."

She paused, looked at him closely. "And?"

He shrugged. "Just saying, we've been living on Cheetos® and Twinkies® from that wrecked truck for what — almost a month? It's getting old — and we're going to be running out of those soon, anyway. If there's a God."

She straightened up, raised one eyebrow and looked at him steadily while she raised her arm, peeled back her sleeve. "Before you start making meal plans, just remember," she said, tapping a tattoo on her forearm. "Force Recon, Kandahar '29."

He looked back, unwavering. "Webelos, Rock Lake, '15. Mom said I was too young to get ink."

There was a moment of silence, then she smiled crookedly. "Okay, just so we understand one another." She squatted now, and shined the light into the cabinet, began shifting more pots and pans, pulling them out and setting them on the floor. "Besides," she added, "you know what they say: 'Do not worry about what you will eat or drink …is life more than food?'"

He snorted. "Not right now, it's not. And besides, who says that? Someone who's never gone hungry, I'll bet."

"Well, that would be Jesus," she answered. "And it's from Matthew 6 — you know: 'See how the flowers of the field grow. They do not labor or spin.' That one."

His eyebrows drew together as he looked down at her, watched her rummage through the cabinet. This was new. "Jesus? Are you a preacher's kid, or something?"

"Something like that." She lay down, then, so she could reach further back, and began pulling out dishes that were covered with a thick coat of dust. "I'm a second year seminary student — I enrolled after I got home. Would've finished, too, if everything hadn't gone to squat."

"Oh. Sorry."

She shrugged again. "Don't be — it's just one of those things. One of those end-of-the-world-as-we-know-it things. But ever since it happened, I've been trying to hang on to Matthew 6. See, Jesus is telling his followers to stop worrying about the things of this world, because God's already given them so much. Don't worry about what you're going to eat, or wear, or where you're going to live. Keep your eyes on God, and God's kingdom."

"So don't worry, be happy?"

"Kind of. Look, do you know about the Israelites and the Exodus? And manna?"

"That's that bread stuff that came to Charlton Heston in the Sinai?"

"Close enough. It's a substance that God sent to them every morning except Sabbath, when he sent a double portion the day before, so they would always have enough to eat. Do you get what that means? It means that out in the middle of a trackless wilderness, God figured out how to provide them with bread every day."

"I wouldn't mind a little bread right now," he said meditatively.

"Shush. Focus. The funny thing is, the Israelites started to complain about it after a while. They started complaining that all they had was bread, instead of being grateful they were getting bread every day."

There was a long silence. Then, "Sort of like complaining about only having snacks for food?" he asked quietly.

She smiled to herself. "You catch on fast." Something caught her eye; she reached back, muttered something under her breath, and pulled out a stiff, desiccated mouse, lobbed it away. She sat for a moment, legs drawn up, arms resting on knees. "The thing is, people have this incredible capacity for getting hung up on what they don't have, instead of being happy with what they do have. We seem to be wired that way — it's part of the brokenness of this world, I think. I know it happens to me, if I let it — so I choose to remember what God's already done for me, rather than fret about the rest."

He looked down at her, offered his hand. "So how's that working for you now?"

She reached up, grabbed his hand and pulled herself up. "Some days are worse than others," she said frankly. "But Jesus didn't say 'don't worry unless things are really bad.'" She looked around the ransacked kitchen. "These folks must've eaten up every scrap of food they had before they left — or passed." They hadn't searched the house, did not know if the former residents remained in another room.

He sighed, nodded. "How inconsiderate of them."

She chuckled. "I know, right?" She leaned back against the counter, frowned, drummed her fingers unconsciously while she stared past him — then slowly stood up straight. *What are the odds?* she thought and took a couple of quick steps across the kitchen to the microwave, yanked the door open.

Her frown disappeared as she turned and held up a pair of heavy plastic pouches. "So, just wondering, how would you feel about —" she turned the pouches, looked at the labels, "— freeze dried stroganoff tonight?"

He grabbed one of the pouches and studied it as though he'd just found buried treasure, turned it over and over in his hand, finally looked at her and smiled. "It's not bread," he said, "but I guess it'll do. It's what we have, right?"

"Now you're getting it," she said, and took the pouch back, stuffed both in her backpack for later. "And, by the way — sorry if I ruined your dinner plans," she added with a mischievous grin.

www.ingramcontent.com/pod-product-compliance
Lightning Source LLC
Chambersburg PA
CBHW031627160426
43196CB00006B/315